Taste of Home's
Chocolate Lover's
Cookbook

Welcome to the Cookbook for People who Consider Chocolate One of the Great Loves of Their Lives!

IF YOU ADORE CHOCOLATE, you probably won't be putting this special collection on the shelf with all your other cookbooks. There are so many dreamy chocolate choices that you could find yourself using this cookbook every day. Why even bother putting it away?

First, let's talk numbers. There are 230 glorious chocolate recipes in *Taste of Home's Chocolate Lover's Cookbook*. That's 28 mouth-watering candies, 30 cookies, 38 bars and brownies, 36 cakes and cheesecakes, 19 ice cream treats and sauces, 30 pies, pudding and mousse and 20 specialty desserts that don't fit easily into a category.

Let's not forget that chocolate is not just for dessert. So we also included 15 breads and muffins, nine snacks and five beverages.

All of the recipes were chosen as the cream of the crop from *Taste of Home*, the most popular cooking magazine in the country, and its sister publications.

Now let's talk flavor. There's milk chocolate, dark chocolate and white chocolate, of course. Then we mixed all that chocolate with other favorites like coffee, peanut butter, raspberry, coconut, caramel, mint, cherry and a variety of nuts.

You'll run out of occasions long before you'll run out of fabulous chocolate recipes to serve. For example:

Having a picnic? Chocolate Malted Cookies (page 28) are for you.

Hosting the boss for a dinner party? Impress him or her with Chocolate Lover's Chiffon Cake (page 52), Chocolate Truffle Cheesecake or Triple Layer Brownie Cake (both recipes on page 50).

Need something for a potluck dinner? Super Brownies (page 36) will win rave reviews.

Are your kids picky eaters? They'll dig right in to Grandma's Chocolate Pudding (page 81).

Want to make something your family would never expect? How about Chocolate Banana Cream Pie (page 81), Chocolate Caramel Pears (page 88) or Black Forest Crepes (page 89)?

Need something for special times like Valentine's Day or Christmas? Something fresh from the kitchen is truly a gift from the heart. Check out Valentine Berries and Cream (page 94), Raspberry Truffles (Page 6) or Triple-Chocolate Quick Bread (page 101).

Well, are you hungry yet? Do you feel a chocolate craving coming on? Then go ahead and get going. You have 230 wonderful recipes ahead of you!

Chocolate Lover's Cookbook

Editor: Jean Steiner
Art Director: Lori Arndt
Food Editor: Janaan Cunningham
Associate Food Editors: Coleen Martin, Diane Werner
Senior Recipe Editor: Sue A. Jurack
Associate Editors: Heidi Reuter Lloyd, Susan Uphill
Food Photography: Rob Hagen, Dan Roberts
Senior Food Photography Artist: Stephanie Marchese
Food Photography Artist: Julie Ferron
Photo Studio Manager: Anne Schimmel
Graphic Art Associates: Ellen Lloyd, Catherine Fletcher
Chairman and Founder: Roy Reiman
President: Tom Curl

©2003 Reiman Media Group, Inc.
5400 S. 60th St., Greendale WI 53129
International Standard Book Number: 0-89821-375-4
Library of Congress Control Number: 2002096802
All rights reserved.
Printed in U.S.A.

Pictured on front cover (clockwise from top right): Chocolate Lover's Chiffon Cake (p. 52), Texas Cake (p. 56), Decadent Fudge Cake (p. 62), Double Chocolate Truffles (p. 10) and Chocolate Macaroon Brownies (p. 47).

Pictured on back cover (clockwise from top right): Chocolate Cookie Muffins (p. 102), English Toffee Bars (p. 7), Monster Chip Cookies (p. 27) and Brownie Caramel Parfaits (p. 70).

PECAN DELIGHTS, PAGE 11

CANDY BAR FUDGE, PAGE 12

ANGEL FOOD CANDY, PAGE 6

DOUBLE CHOCOLATE TRUFFLES, PAGE 10

Candies

Chocolate Almond Brittle

(Pictured above)

Here in Kern County, there are thousands of acres of almond orchards. I like to experiment with recipes—always trying to come up with something new. This candy is the result of altering, adding and a lot of taste-testing (somebody had to do it!). I think it turned out rather well.

—Pat Parsons, Bakersfield, California

> 1 cup sugar
> 1/2 cup light corn syrup
> 1/8 teaspoon salt
> 1 cup coarsely chopped almonds
> 1 tablespoon butter (no substitutes)
> 1 teaspoon vanilla extract
> 1-1/2 teaspoons baking soda
> 3/4 pound chocolate candy coating

In a 1-1/2-qt. microwave-safe bowl, combine sugar, corn syrup and salt; mix well. Microwave on high for 4 minutes. Stir in almonds; microwave on high for 4 minutes. Add the butter and vanilla; microwave on high for 1-1/2 minutes. Stir in baking soda. As soon as the mixture foams, quickly pour onto a greased metal baking sheet.

Cool completely. Break into 2-in. pieces. Melt candy coating in a double boiler or microwave oven. Dip one side of brittle in chocolate; place on waxed paper to harden. Store in an airtight container. **Yield:** about 1 pound.

Editor's Note: This recipe was tested using a 700-watt microwave.

Angel Food Candy

(Pictured on page 4)

It was my dad who inspired me to first try making this candy. He remembered it from when he was a boy. The ultimate compliment was when he told me my version tasted even better!—Shelly Matthys, New Richmond, Wisconsin

> 1 cup sugar
> 1 cup dark corn syrup
> 1 tablespoon white vinegar
> 1 tablespoon baking soda
> 1 pound chocolate candy coating, melted

In a heavy saucepan, combine sugar, corn syrup and vinegar. Cook over medium heat, stirring constantly, until sugar dissolves. Cook without stirring until the temperature reaches 300° (hard-crack stage) on a candy thermometer. Do not overcook. Remove from the heat and quickly stir in baking soda. Pour into a buttered 13-in. x 9-in. x 2-in. pan. Do not spread candy; mixture will not fill pan. When cool, break into bite-size pieces. Dip into melted chocolate; place on waxed paper until firm. Store in an airtight container. **Yield:** 1-1/2 pounds.

Editor's Note: We recommend that you test your candy thermometer before each use by bringing water to a boil; the thermometer should read 212°. Adjust your recipe temperature up or down based on your test.

Raspberry Truffles

(Pictured below)

As everyone in my neighborhood knows, Christmas is my favorite time of year. I make many cookies, cakes and candies—including this easy but elegant recipe—to give to relatives and friends. —Helen Vail, Glenside, Pennsylvania

> 1 tablespoon butter (no substitutes)
> 2 tablespoons whipping cream
> 1-1/3 cups semisweet chocolate chips
> 7-1/2 teaspoons seedless raspberry jam
> 6 ounces white *or* dark chocolate candy coating
> 2 tablespoons shortening

In a heavy saucepan, combine butter, cream and chocolate chips. Cook over low heat for 4-5 minutes or until chocolate is melted. Remove from the heat; stir in jam until combined. Transfer to a small freezer container; cover and freeze for 20 minutes. Drop by teaspoonfuls onto a foil-lined baking sheet. Freeze for 15 minutes. Roll into balls; freeze until very firm.

In a microwave oven or heavy saucepan, melt candy coating and shortening, stirring often. Cool slightly; spoon over balls. Place on a wire rack over waxed paper. Let stand for 15 minutes or until firm. Refrigerate in an airtight container. **Yield:** 4 dozen.

English Toffee Bars

(Pictured above)

My mother and I get together every Christmas to make this delicious chocolate-coated toffee. It's a tradition I plan to continue with my own daughters. —Dianne Brooks
Augusta, Kansas

    1 tablespoon plus 1-3/4 cups butter
      (no substitutes), softened, *divided*
    2 cups sugar
    1 tablespoon light corn syrup
    1 cup chopped pecans
  1/4 teaspoon salt
    1 pound milk chocolate candy coating

Butter a 15-in. x 10-in. x 1-in. pan with 1 tablespoon butter; set aside. In a heavy saucepan, melt remaining butter. Add sugar and corn syrup; cook and stir over medium heat until a candy thermometer reads 295° (soft-crack stage). Remove from heat; stir in pecans and salt. Quickly pour into prepared pan. Let stand 5 minutes.

Using a sharp knife, score into squares; cut along scored lines. Let stand at room temperature until cool. Separate into squares, using a sharp knife if necessary. In a microwave oven or heavy saucepan, melt candy coating, stirring often. Dip squares, one at a time, in coating. Place on waxed paper until set. **Yield:** 2-1/4 pounds.

Editor's Note: We recommend that you test your candy thermometer before each use by bringing water to a boil; the thermometer should read 212°. Adjust your recipe temperature up or down based on your test.

Cashew Caramel Fudge

A pretty plate of this yummy confection makes a great present! Cashews and caramel are such a delicious combination. I especially enjoy making this fudge for a holiday treat. —Cathy Grubelnik, Raton, New Mexico

    2 teaspoons plus 1/2 cup butter (no substitutes),
      softened, *divided*
    1 can (5 ounces) evaporated milk
2-1/2 cups sugar
    2 cups (12 ounces) semisweet chocolate chips
    1 jar (7 ounces) marshmallow creme
   24 caramels, quartered
  3/4 cup salted cashew halves
    1 teaspoon vanilla extract

Line a 9-in. square pan with foil; butter the foil with 2 teaspoons butter. Set aside. In a large heavy saucepan, combine milk, sugar and remaining butter. Cook and stir over medium heat until sugar is dissolved. Bring to a rapid boil; boil for 5 minutes, stirring constantly.

Remove from the heat; stir in chocolate chips and marshmallow creme until melted. Fold in caramels, cashews and vanilla; mix well. Pour into prepared pan. Cool. Remove from pan and cut into 1-in. squares. Store at room temperature. **Yield:** about 3 pounds.

Maple Peanut Delights

(Pictured below)

This wonderful candy recipe makes a big batch—enough to fill several Christmas gift boxes and still have treats left for my family. —Katie Stutzman, Goshen, Indiana

    1 package (8 ounces) cream cheese, softened
  1/2 cup butter (no substitutes), softened
    6 cups confectioners' sugar
    1 teaspoon maple flavoring
    2 pounds dark chocolate candy coating
    1 cup chopped peanuts

In a mixing bowl, beat cream cheese, butter, confectioners' sugar and maple flavoring until smooth. Cover and refrigerate for 1 hour. Shape into 1-in. balls. In a microwave oven or heavy saucepan, melt candy coating, stirring often. Dip balls in coating; sprinkle with peanuts. Place on waxed paper-lined baking sheets. Refrigerate. **Yield:** about 8 dozen.

Nutty Chocolate Marshmallow Puffs

(Pictured at right)

We like to do things BIG here in Texas, so don't expect a dainty little barely-a-bite truffle from this surprising recipe. Folks are delighted to discover a big fluffy marshmallow inside the chocolate and nut coating. —Pat Ball
Abilene, Texas

2 cups milk chocolate chips
1 can (14 ounces) sweetened condensed milk
1 jar (7 ounces) marshmallow creme
40 large marshmallows
4 cups coarsely chopped pecans (about 1 pound)

In a microwave oven or heavy saucepan, heat the chocolate chips, milk and marshmallow creme just until melted; stir until smooth (mixture will be thick). With tongs, immediately dip marshmallows, one at a time, in the chocolate mixture. Shake off excess chocolate; quickly roll in pecans. Place on waxed paper-lined baking sheets. (Reheat chocolate mixture if necessary for easier coating.) Refrigerate until firm. Refrigerate in an airtight container. **Yield:** 40 candies.

Fondant-Filled Candies

(Pictured below)

Here's an easy way to make two unique candies from one basic recipe! Half of the fondant is flavored with mint for the centers of peppermint patties. Then you mix a little maraschino cherry juice with the rest of the fondant and use it to "wrap" cherries before dipping them in chocolate.
—Debbi Loney, Central City, Kentucky

2/3 cup sweetened condensed milk
1 tablespoon light corn syrup
4-1/2 to 5 cups confectioners' sugar
2 to 4 drops peppermint oil*
2-1/2 pounds dark chocolate candy coating, *divided*
1 jar (16 ounces) maraschino cherries

In a mixing bowl, combine milk and corn syrup. Gradually beat in confectioners' sugar (mixture will be stiff). Divide into two portions.

For peppermint patties, add the peppermint oil to one portion. Shape 1/2 teaspoonfuls into balls and flatten. In a microwave oven or heavy saucepan, melt 1 pound of candy coating, stirring often. With a slotted spoon, dip peppermint disks in coating; place on waxed paper to harden. Refrigerate in an airtight container.

For chocolate-covered cherries, drain cherries, reserving 3 tablespoons of juice; set cherries aside. Combine juice with remaining fondant. Add additional confectioners' sugar if necessary to form a stiff mixture. Roll into 1-in. balls; flatten into 2-in. circles. Wrap each circle around a cherry; carefully shape into a ball. Place on waxed paper-lined baking sheets. Cover loosely. Melt remaining candy coating; dip cherries. Place on waxed paper to harden. Refrigerate in an airtight container for 1-2 weeks for candy to ripen and center to soften. **Yield:** 4-1/2 dozen.

***Editor's Note:** Peppermint oil can be found in some pharmacies or at kitchen and cake decorating supply stores.

Chocolate Pecan Caramels

I haven't missed a year making this candy for the holidays since a friend gave me the recipe in 1964! It tastes like my favorite caramel pecan candies. —June Humphrey
Strongsville, Ohio

1 tablespoon plus 1 cup butter (no substitutes), softened, *divided*
1-1/2 cups coarsely chopped pecans, toasted
1 cup (6 ounces) semisweet chocolate chips
2 cups packed brown sugar
1 cup light corn syrup
1/4 cup water

1 can (14 ounces) sweetened condensed milk
2 teaspoons vanilla extract

Line a 13-in. x 9-in. x 2-in. pan with foil; butter the foil with 1 tablespoon butter. Sprinkle with pecans and chocolate chips; set aside. In a heavy saucepan over medium heat, melt remaining butter. Add brown sugar, corn syrup and water. Cook and stir until mixture comes to a boil. Stir in milk. Cook, stirring constantly, until a candy thermometer reads 248° (firm-ball stage). Remove from heat and stir in vanilla. Pour into prepared pan (do not scrape saucepan). Cool completely before cutting. **Yield:** about 2-1/2 pounds (about 6-3/4 dozen).

Editor's Note: We recommend that you test your candy thermometer before each use by bringing water to a boil; the thermometer should read 212°. Adjust your recipe temperature up or down based on your test.

Cranberry Almond Bark

The addition of dried cranberries makes this almond bark extra special. —*Elizabeth Hodges*
Regina Beach, Saskatchewan

8 squares (1 ounce *each*) white baking chocolate
3 squares (1 ounce *each*) semisweet chocolate
3/4 cup whole blanched almonds, toasted
3/4 cup dried cranberries

In a microwave oven or heavy saucepan, melt white chocolate; set aside. Repeat with semisweet chocolate. Stir almonds and cranberries into white chocolate. Thinly spread onto a waxed paper-lined baking sheet. Drizzle semisweet chocolate over the white chocolate. Cut through with a knife to swirl. Chill until firm. Break into pieces. Refrigerate in an airtight container. **Yield:** 1 pound.

Chocolate Mint Candy

(Pictured below)

I never made candy before until I tried this easy recipe. Now my family expects it every holiday and I'm happy to oblige. —*Kendra Pedersen, Battle Ground, Washington*

2 cups (12 ounces) semisweet chocolate chips
1 can (14 ounces) sweetened condensed milk, *divided*
2 teaspoons vanilla extract
6 ounces white candy coating
2 to 3 teaspoons peppermint extract
3 drops green food coloring

In a heavy saucepan, melt chocolate chips with 1 cup milk. Remove from the heat; stir in vanilla. Spread half into a waxed paper-lined 8-in. square pan; chill for 10 minutes or until firm.

Meanwhile, in a heavy saucepan over low heat, cook and stir candy coating with remaining milk until coating is melted and mixture is smooth. Stir in peppermint extract and food coloring. Spread over bottom layer; chill for 10 minutes or until firm. Warm remaining chocolate mixture if necessary; spread over mint layer. Chill for 2 hours or until firm. Remove from pan; cut into 1-in. squares. **Yield:** about 2 pounds.

S'more Clusters

(Pictured above)

Our two sons love to help me break up the chocolate and graham crackers for these tasty treats—that way, they can tell their friends they made them! The chocolaty clusters taste just like s'mores, but without the gooey mess.
—*Kathy Schmittler, Sterling Heights, Michigan*

6 milk chocolate candy bars (1.55 ounces *each*), broken into pieces
1-1/2 teaspoons vegetable oil
2 cups miniature marshmallows
8 whole graham crackers, broken into bite-size pieces

In a large microwave-safe bowl, toss chocolate and oil. Microwave, uncovered, at 50% power for 1-1/2 to 2 minutes or until chocolate is melted, stirring once. Stir in marshmallows and graham crackers. Spoon into paper-lined muffin cups (about 1/3 cup each). Refrigerate for 1 hour or until firm. **Yield:** 1 dozen.

Editor's Note: This recipe was tested in an 850-watt microwave.

Maine Potato Candy

(Pictured above)

Years ago, folks in Maine ate potatoes daily and used left-overs in bread, doughnuts and candy. —Barbara Allen Chelmsford, Massachusetts

   4 cups confectioners' sugar
   4 cups flaked coconut
   3/4 cup cold mashed potatoes (without added milk
      or butter)
1-1/2 teaspoons vanilla extract
   1/2 teaspoon salt
   1 pound dark candy coating

In a large bowl, combine the first five ingredients. Line a 9-in. square pan with foil; butter the foil. Spread coconut mixture into pan. Cover and chill overnight. Cut into 2-in. x 1-in. rectangles. Cover and freeze. In a microwave oven or double boiler, melt candy coating. Dip bars in coating; place on waxed paper to harden. Store in an airtight container. **Yield:** 2 pounds.

Double Chocolate Truffles

(Pictured on front cover and on page 4)

Here's a delicious holiday treat that's very rich and choco-laty. I like to make extra and give them as homemade Christmas presents. —Ruth Gordon, Lakewood, New York

1-1/3 cups semisweet chocolate chips
   1/3 cup whipping cream
   3 tablespoons butter (no substitutes)
   1 teaspoon vanilla extract
   1 cup (6 ounces) vanilla *or* white chips
   2 tablespoons shortening, *divided*
   1 cup milk chocolate chips

In a microwave-safe bowl, heat chocolate chips, whipping cream and butter on medium for about 2-3 minutes. Stir, then heat an additional 2-3 minutes or until melted. Add vanilla; cool. Refrigerate until almost solid but still workable (about 1 hour). Shape into 1/2-in. balls. Melt white chips and 1 tablespoon shortening in the microwave

oven. Dip balls and set on waxed paper to dry. Melt milk chocolate chips and remaining shortening; dip balls again and allow to dry. **Yield:** 2-1/2 dozen.

Four-Chip Fudge

(Pictured below)

I stir up this wonderful creamy fudge every Christmas. My friend Marlene gave me the recipe years ago. Flavored with four different kinds of chips, this is the best fudge I've ever tasted! —Delores Wigginton, Prudenville, Michigan

1-1/2 teaspoons plus 3/4 cup butter (no substitutes),
      divided
   1 can (14 ounces) sweetened condensed milk
   3 tablespoons milk
   1 package (12 ounces) semisweet chocolate chips
   1 package (11-1/2 ounces) milk chocolate chips
   1 package (10 ounces) peanut butter chips
   1 cup (6 ounces) butterscotch chips
   1 jar (7 ounces) marshmallow creme
   1/2 teaspoon almond extract
   1/2 teaspoon vanilla extract
   1 cup chopped walnuts

Line a 13-in. x 9-in. x 2-in. pan with foil and grease the foil with 1-1/2 teaspoons of butter; set aside. In a large heavy saucepan, melt the remaining butter over low heat. Add the next six ingredients. Cook and stir constantly until smooth. Mixture will first appear separated; continue stirring until fully blended. Remove from the heat; stir in the marshmallow creme and extracts until well blended. Stir in nuts.

Spread into prepared pan. Refrigerate until set. Lift out of pan and remove foil; cut into squares. Store in the refrigerator. **Yield:** about 4-1/2 pounds.

Mocha Truffles

(Pictured at right)

Nothing compares to the melt-in-your-mouth flavor of these truffles...or to the simplicity of the recipe.
—*Stacy Abell, Olathe, Kansas*

- 2 packages (12 ounces *each*) semisweet chocolate chips
- 1 package (8 ounces) cream cheese, softened
- 3 tablespoons instant coffee granules
- 2 teaspoons water
- 1 pound dark chocolate candy coating
- White candy coating, optional

In a microwave-safe bowl or double boiler, melt chocolate chips. Add cream cheese, coffee and water; mix well. Chill until firm enough to shape. Shape into 1-in. balls and place on a waxed paper-lined baking sheet. Chill for 1-2 hours or until firm. Melt dark chocolate coating in microwave-safe bowl or double boiler. Dip balls and place on waxed paper to harden. If desired, melt white coating and drizzle over truffles. **Yield:** about 5-1/2 dozen.

Editor's Note: Truffles can be frozen for several months before dipping in chocolate. Thaw in the refrigerator before dipping.

Perfect Peppermint Patties

(Pictured below)

Calling for just a few ingredients, this is one candy that's simple to prepare. I make lots of different candy at Christmas to give as gifts. It can be time-consuming, but worth it to see the delight it brings to people. —*Joanne Adams Bath, Maine*

- 1 package (1 pound) confectioners' sugar
- 3 tablespoons butter (no substitutes), softened
- 2 to 3 teaspoons peppermint extract
- 1/2 teaspoon vanilla extract
- 1/4 cup evaporated milk
- 2 cups (12 ounces) semisweet chocolate chips
- 2 tablespoons shortening

In a bowl, combine first four ingredients. Add milk and mix well. Roll into 1-in. balls and place on a waxed paper-lined baking sheet. Flatten with a glass to 1/4 in. Cover and freeze for 30 minutes. In a double boiler or microwave-safe bowl, melt chocolate chips and shortening. Dip patties; place on waxed paper to harden. **Yield:** about 5 dozen.

Pecan Delights

(Pictured on page 4)

A relative visiting from Oklahoma brought these and the recipe with her. These candies have become a holiday favorite to both make and eat! —*Linda Jonsson Marion, Ohio*

- 2-1/4 cups packed brown sugar
- 1 cup butter (no substitutes)
- 1 cup light corn syrup
- 1/8 teaspoon salt
- 1 can (14 ounces) sweetened condensed milk
- 1 teaspoon vanilla extract
- 1-1/2 pounds whole pecans
- 1 cup (6 ounces) semisweet chocolate chips
- 1 cup milk chocolate chips
- 2 tablespoons shortening

In a large saucepan, combine the first four ingredients. Cook over medium heat until all sugar is dissolved. Gradually add milk and mix well. Continue cooking until candy thermometer reads 248° (firm-ball stage). Remove from the heat; stir in vanilla until blended. Fold in the pecans. Drop by tablespoonfuls onto a greased or parchment-lined baking sheet. Chill until firm. Loosen from paper. Melt chocolate chips and shortening in a microwave-safe bowl or double boiler. Drizzle over each cluster. Cool. **Yield:** about 4 dozen.

Editor's Note: We recommend that you test your candy thermometer before each use by bringing water to a boil; the thermometer should read 212°. Adjust your recipe temperature up or down based on your test.

Three-Chocolate Fudge

(Pictured at right)

I make this fudge at Christmastime to give to friends and neighbors. That tradition started years ago when I made more candy than my husband, three sons and I could eat, so we shared it. It's a tasty tradition I'm glad to continue.
— Betty Grantham, Hanceville, Alabama

3-1/3 cups sugar
   1 cup butter (no substitutes)
   1 cup packed dark brown sugar
   1 can (12 ounces) evaporated milk
 32 large marshmallows, halved
   2 cups (12 ounces) semisweet chocolate chips
   2 milk chocolate candy bars (7 ounces *each*), broken
   2 squares (1 ounce *each*) semisweet chocolate, chopped
   1 teaspoon vanilla extract
   2 cups chopped pecans

In a large saucepan, combine the first four ingredients. Cook and stir over medium heat until sugar is dissolved. Bring to a rapid boil; boil for 5 minutes, stirring constantly.

Remove from the heat; stir in marshmallows until melted. Stir in chocolate chips until melted. Add chocolate bars and baking chocolate; stir until melted. Fold in vanilla and pecans; mix well. Pour into a greased 15-in. x 10-in. x 1-in. pan. Chill until firm. Cut into squares. **Yield:** 5-1/2 pounds.

Orange Chocolate Meltaways

(Pictured below)

The terrific combination of chocolate and orange makes these some of the best truffles I've ever had. As holiday gifts, they're showstoppers. I have little time to cook, but when I do, I like to "get fancy". In this case, "fancy" doesn't have to be difficult. — Lori Kostecki, Wausau, Wisconsin

   1 package (11-1/2 ounces) milk chocolate chips
   1 cup (6 ounces) semisweet chocolate chips
 3/4 cup whipping cream
   1 teaspoon grated orange peel
2-1/2 teaspoons orange extract
1-1/2 cups finely chopped toasted pecans
COATING:
   1 cup milk chocolate chips
   2 tablespoons shortening

Place chocolate chips in a mixing bowl; set aside. In a saucepan, bring cream and orange peel to a gentle boil; immediately pour over chips. Let stand for 1 minute; whisk until smooth. Add the extract. Cover and chill for 35 minutes or until mixture begins to thicken. Beat for 10-15 seconds or just until mixture lightens in color (do not overbeat).

Spoon rounded teaspoonfuls onto waxed paper-lined baking sheets. Cover and chill for 5 minutes. Gently shape into balls; roll half in pecans. In a microwave oven or double boiler, melt chocolate and shortening; stir until smooth. Dip remaining balls in chocolate. Place on waxed paper to harden. Store in the refrigerator. **Yield:** 6 dozen.

Candy Bar Fudge

(Pictured on page 4)

My manager at work, who knows I like to try new treat recipes, shared this one with me. Packed with nuts and caramel, it's like a candy bar. —Lois Zigarac
Rochester Hills, Michigan

1/2 cup butter (no substitutes)
1/3 cup baking cocoa
1/4 cup packed brown sugar
1/4 cup milk
3-1/2 cups confectioners' sugar
   1 teaspoon vanilla extract
 30 caramels, unwrapped

1 tablespoon water
2 cups salted peanuts
1/2 cup semisweet chocolate chips
1/2 cup milk chocolate chips

In a microwave-safe bowl, combine the butter, cocoa, brown sugar and milk. Microwave on high until mixture boils, about 3 minutes. Stir in confectioners' sugar and vanilla. Pour into a greased 8-in. square pan.

In another microwave-safe bowl, heat caramels and water on high for 2 minutes or until melted. Stir in peanuts; spread over chocolate layer. Microwave chocolate chips on high for 1 minute or until melted; spread over caramel layer. Chill until firm. **Yield:** 2-3/4 pounds.

Editor's Note: This recipe was tested using a 700-watt microwave.

True Love Truffles

(Pictured above right)

A few years ago, I began giving these smooth, minty truffles in tins as Christmas gifts. Now I can't go a year without sharing them. They also make a perfect Valentine's treat. —Kim Weiesnbach, Claremore, Oklahoma

1-1/2 cups sugar
  3/4 cup butter (no substitutes)
    1 can (5 ounces) evaporated milk
    2 packages (4.67 ounces *each*) mint Andes candies
      (56 pieces total)
    1 jar (7 ounces) marshmallow creme
    1 teaspoon vanilla extract
  22 ounces white baking chocolate, *divided*
  1/2 cup semisweet chocolate chips
Green food coloring, optional

In a heavy saucepan, combine sugar, butter and milk. Bring to a boil over medium heat, stirring constantly. Reduce heat; cook and stir until a candy thermometer reads 236° (soft-ball stage). Remove from the heat. Stir in candies until melted and mixture is well blended. Stir in marshmallow creme and vanilla until smooth.

Spread into a buttered 15-in. x 10-in. x 1-in. pan; cover and refrigerate for 1 hour. Cut into 96 pieces; roll each into a ball (mixture will be soft). Place on a waxed paper-lined baking sheet. In a heavy saucepan or microwave-safe bowl, melt 18 oz. of white chocolate and chocolate chips. Dip balls in melted chocolate; place on waxed paper to harden. Melt the remaining white chocolate; add food coloring if desired. Drizzle over truffles. Store in an airtight container. **Yield:** 8 dozen.

Editor's Note: We recommend that you test your candy thermometer before each use by bringing water to a boil; the thermometer should read 212°. Adjust your recipe temperature up or down based on your test.

Chocolate Peanut Sweeties

(Pictured at left)

Inspired by my passion for peanut butter and chocolate, I combined a trusted recipe for peanut butter eggs with the salty crunch of pretzels. —Gina Kintigh
Connellsville, Pennsylvania

    1 cup peanut butter*
  1/2 cup butter (no substitutes), softened
    3 cups confectioners' sugar
    5 dozen miniature pretzel twists (about 3 cups)
1-1/2 cups milk chocolate chips
    1 tablespoon vegetable oil

In a mixing bowl, beat peanut butter and butter until smooth. Beat in confectioners' sugar until combined. Shape into 1-in. balls; press one on each pretzel. Place on waxed paper-lined baking sheets. Refrigerate until peanut butter mixture is firm, about 1 hour.

In a microwave-safe bowl or heavy saucepan, melt chocolate chips and oil. Dip the peanut butter ball into chocolate. Return to baking sheet, pretzel side down. Refrigerate for at least 30 minutes before serving. Store in the refrigerator. **Yield:** 5 dozen.

*Editor's Note: Reduced-fat or generic-brand peanut butter is not recommended for use in this recipe.

Chocolate Easter Eggs

(Pictured above)

No store-bought Easter candy can compare to Mom's home-made chocolate-covered eggs. The heavenly centers have peanut butter, coconut and walnuts. These rich candies just melt in your mouth. —Ruth Seitz
Columbus Junction, Iowa

- 3/4 cup chunky peanut butter
- 1/4 cup butter (no substitutes), softened
- 1 cup flaked coconut
- 1/2 cup finely chopped walnuts
- 1-1/2 to 2 cups confectioners' sugar, *divided*
- 2 cups (12 ounces) semisweet chocolate chips
- 2 tablespoons shortening

In a mixing bowl, cream peanut butter and butter until well mixed. Fold in coconut, nuts and 1 cup sugar; mix well. Sprinkle some of the remaining sugar on a board.

Turn peanut butter mixture onto board; knead in enough of the remaining sugar until mixture holds its shape when formed. Shape into small egg-shaped pieces. Cover and chill for 1 hour. In a double boiler over hot water, melt chocolate chips and shortening, stirring until smooth. Dip eggs; place on waxed paper to harden. Chill. **Yield:** 2 dozen.

Sweet Peanut Treats

We sold tempting bars almost like these at the refreshment stand at a Minnesota state park where I worked in the '70s, and they were a favorite of employees and visitors alike. Now I make this recipe when I want to serve a special treat. —Phyllis Smith, Olympia, Washington

- 2 cups (12 ounces) semisweet chocolate chips
- 2 cups (12 ounces) butterscotch chips
- 1 jar (18 ounces) creamy peanut butter

- 1 cup butter (no substitutes)
- 1 can (5 ounces) evaporated milk
- 1/4 cup vanilla cook-and-serve pudding mix
- 7-1/2 cups (2 pounds) confectioners' sugar
- 1 pound salted peanuts

In the top of a double boiler over simmering water, melt chocolate chips, butterscotch chips and peanut butter; stir until smooth. Spread half into a greased 15-in. x 10-in. x 1-in. pan. Chill until firm.

Meanwhile, in a saucepan, bring butter, milk and pudding mix to a boil. Cook and stir for 2 minutes. Remove from the heat; add confectioners' sugar and beat until smooth. Spread over chocolate mixture in pan. Stir peanuts into remaining chocolate mixture; mix well. Carefully spread over pudding layer. Chill. Cut into 1-in. squares. **Yield:** 10 dozen.

Three-Chip English Toffee

(Pictured below)

With its melt-in-your-mouth texture and scrumptiously rich flavor, this is the ultimate toffee! Drizzled on top are three different kinds of melted chips, plus a sprinkling of walnuts. Packaged in colorful tins, these pretty pieces make great gifts. —Lana Petfield, Richmond, Virginia

- 1/2 teaspoon plus 2 cups butter (no substitutes), *divided*
- 2 cups sugar
- 1 cup slivered almonds
- 1 cup milk chocolate chips
- 1 cup chopped walnuts
- 1/2 cup semisweet chocolate chips
- 1/2 cup vanilla *or* white chips
- 1-1/2 teaspoons shortening

Butter a 15-in. x 10-in. x 1-in. pan with 1/2 teaspoon butter. In a heavy saucepan over medium-low heat, bring

sugar and remaining butter to a boil, stirring constantly. Cover and cook for 2-3 minutes.

Uncover; add almonds. Cook and stir with a clean spoon until a candy thermometer reads 300° (hard-crack stage) and mixture is golden brown. Pour into prepared pan (do not scrape sides of saucepan). Surface will be buttery. Cool for 1-2 minutes. Sprinkle with milk chocolate chips. Let stand for 1-2 minutes; spread chocolate over the top. Sprinkle with walnuts; press down gently with the back of a spoon. Chill for 10 minutes.

In a microwave oven or heavy saucepan, melt semisweet chips; stir until smooth. Drizzle over walnuts. Refrigerate for 10 minutes. Melt vanilla chips and shortening; stir until smooth. Drizzle over walnuts. Cover and refrigerate for 1-2 hours. Break into pieces. **Yield:** about 2-1/2 pounds.

Editor's Note: We recommend that you test your candy thermometer before each use by bringing water to a boil; the thermometer should read 212°. Adjust your recipe temperature up or down based on your test. If toffee separates during cooking, add 1/2 cup hot water and stir vigorously. Bring back up to 300° and proceed as recipe directs.

Chocolate Peanut Butter Bars

My daughter won first place in a contest with this candy, which I make at Christmastime. It melts in your mouth!
—*Mary Esther Holloway, Bowerston, Ohio*

   3 cups sugar
   1 cup light corn syrup
1/2 cup water
   1 jar (18 ounces) creamy peanut butter, melted
1-1/2 pounds milk chocolate candy coating

Take a Sweet Dip—in Chocolate!

THERE'S no better way to sweeten a celebration for the holidays than with chocolate-covered goodies!

What's more, doing so is a cinch, according to our Test Kitchen home economists. To help you plunge into the process, they've stirred up easy-to-follow instructions right here:

In a microwave oven or heavy saucepan, melt 1 cup of semisweet or milk chocolate chips and 1 tablespoon shortening. Stir until the mixture is smooth.

Place cookies, candies or fruit on a fork; dip one at a time into the melted chocolate and drain the excess. Place on waxed paper-lined baking sheets and refrigerate for about 1 hour or until the chocolate is hard.

Store the chocolate-dipped treats in an airtight container in a cool dark place.

In a large heavy saucepan, combine sugar, corn syrup and water. Cook and stir over low heat until sugar is dissolved; bring to a full rolling boil. Boil, stirring constantly, until a candy thermometer reads 290° (soft-crack stage). Meanwhile, place melted peanut butter in a large greased heat-proof bowl. Pour hot syrup over peanut butter; stir quickly until blended.

Pour onto a well-buttered baking sheet; cover with a piece of buttered waxed paper. Roll mixture into a 14-in. x 12-in. rectangle. While warm, cut into 1-1/2-in. x 1-in. bars using a buttered pizza cutter or knife. Cool completely. Melt candy coating; dip bars and place on waxed paper to harden. **Yield:** 6 dozen.

Editor's Note: We recommend that you test your candy thermometer before each use by bringing water to a boil; the thermometer should read 212°. Adjust your recipe temperature up or down based on your test.

Peanut Clusters

(Pictured at left)

My husband, Greg, likes to mix up a batch of these treats with the kids. —*Deb Darr, Falls City, Oregon*

   4 ounces milk chocolate candy coating
   4 ounces white candy coating
   1 can (16 ounces) salted peanuts
     (about 2-1/2 cups)

In a microwave oven, melt candy coatings, stirring often until blended. Stir in the peanuts until coated. Drop by tablespoonfuls onto a waxed paper-lined baking sheet. Refrigerate until serving. **Yield:** about 3 dozen.

CHOCOLATE WAFFLE COOKIES, PAGE 20

CHOCOLATE MARSHMALLOW
COOKIES, PAGE 22

CHOCOLATE SURPRISE COOKIES,
PAGE 18

OAT-RAGEOUS CHOCOLATE CHIP COOKIES,
PAGE 21

Cookies

Chocolate–Covered Cherry Cookies

(Pictured above)

I always make these cookies for family gatherings, and they never last long. —Marie Kinyon, Mason, Michigan

1/2 cup butter *or* margarine
1 cup sugar
1 egg
1-1/2 teaspoons vanilla extract
1-1/2 cups all-purpose flour
1/2 cup baking cocoa
1/4 teaspoon salt
1/4 teaspoon baking powder
1/4 teaspoon baking soda
48 maraschino cherries, blotted dry
FROSTING:
1 cup (6 ounces) semisweet chocolate chips
1/2 cup sweetened condensed milk
1 to 3 teaspoons maraschino cherry juice

In a mixing bowl, cream butter and sugar until fluffy; beat in egg and vanilla. Combine the dry ingredients; gradually add to creamed mixture (batter will be very firm). Shape into 1 in. balls, and place on ungreased baking sheets. Push one cherry halfway into each ball.

For frosting, melt chocolate chips in milk in a small saucepan over low heat, stirring constantly. Remove from the heat; add cherry juice and stir until smooth. Spoon 1 teaspoon of frosting over each cherry (the frosting will spread over cookie during baking). Bake at 350° for 10-12 minutes. Cool on wire racks. **Yield:** 4 dozen.

Chocolate Surprise Cookies

(Pictured on page 16)

Chocolate and peanut butter are popular with our clan, so I roll them together in this recipe. It's fun watching folks' faces when they bite into the middle. —Grace Crary West Linn, Oregon

3/4 cup peanut butter*
3/4 cup confectioners' sugar

CHOCOLATE DOUGH:
1/2 cup butter *or* margarine, softened
1/4 cup peanut butter
1/2 cup sugar
1/2 cup packed brown sugar
1 egg white
1 teaspoon vanilla extract
1-1/2 cups all-purpose flour
1/2 cup baking cocoa
1/2 teaspoon baking soda
ICING:
2 tablespoons shortening
1 cup confectioners' sugar
1/4 teaspoon vanilla extract
1 to 2 tablespoons milk

In a mixing bowl, cream peanut butter and confectioners' sugar until smooth. Roll into thirty 3/4-in. balls. Cover and refrigerate for 30 minutes. Meanwhile, in a mixing bowl, cream butter, peanut butter and sugars. Beat in egg white and vanilla. Combine flour, cocoa and baking soda; gradually add to creamed mixture. Roll into thirty 1-1/2-in. balls.

Using floured hands, flatten chocolate balls and shape one around each peanut butter ball, sealing edges. Place 2 in. apart on greased baking sheets. Flatten with a glass dipped in sugar. Bake at 375° for 7-9 minutes or until cookies are set and tops are cracked. Cool for 1 minute before removing to wire racks.

For icing, in a small mixing bowl, cream shortening and confectioners' sugar. Beat in vanilla and enough milk to reach spreading consistency. Spoon into a resealable plastic bag or pastry bag; cut a small hole in corner of bag. Pipe icing over cookies in a zigzag pattern. **Yield:** 2-1/2 dozen.

*Editor's Note: Reduced-fat or generic brands of peanut butter are not recommended for this recipe.

Sour Cream Chocolate Cookies

(Pictured below)

These soft cookies can easily be altered to make several varieties—I've added everything from mints to macadamia nuts to them. —Tina Sawchuk, Ardmore, Alberta

1/2 cup butter *or* margarine, softened
3/4 cup sugar
1/2 cup packed brown sugar
1 egg
1/2 cup sour cream
1 teaspoon vanilla extract
1-3/4 cups all-purpose flour
1/2 cup baking cocoa
1 teaspoon baking powder
1/2 teaspoon baking soda
1/4 teaspoon salt
1 cup (6 ounces) semisweet chocolate chips
1/2 cup vanilla *or* white chips

In a mixing bowl, cream butter and sugars. Beat in egg, sour cream and vanilla. Combine dry ingredients; gradually add to the creamed mixture. Stir in chips.

Drop by rounded tablespoonfuls 2 in. apart onto greased baking sheets. Bake at 350° for 12-15 minutes or until set. Cool for 2 minutes before removing to wire racks to cool completely. **Yield:** about 3 dozen.

Chocolate Meringues

(Pictured above)

These cookies are great for fancy occasions, but easy enough to make as a snack. My grandma was an avid baker, known in her neighborhood as the "cookie lady". With 18 nieces and nephews, I'm carrying on her tradition.
—Nancy Grace, San Diego, California

1 cup (6 ounces) semisweet chocolate chips
2 egg whites
1/4 teaspoon cream of tartar
1/8 teaspoon salt
1/2 cup sugar
1/2 teaspoon white vinegar
1/2 teaspoon vanilla *or* almond extract
1/2 cup flaked coconut
1/4 cup chopped almonds

In a microwave oven or heavy saucepan, melt chocolate chips and stir until smooth; set aside. In a mixing bowl, beat egg whites, cream of tartar and salt until soft peaks

form. Add sugar, 1 tablespoon at a time, beating until stiff peaks form, about 5 minutes. Beat in vinegar and vanilla. Fold in melted chocolate until combined; fold in coconut and almonds.

Drop by tablespoonfuls 2 in. apart onto lightly greased baking sheets. Bake at 350° for 10-11 minutes or until firm. Remove to wire racks to cool. Store in an airtight container. **Yield:** about 2-1/2 dozen.

White Chocolate Oatmeal Cookies

(Pictured below)

My sons and grandsons manage our ranch…and they always seem to have one hand in the cookie jar—especially when I bake these crunchy morsels!
—Edith Pluhar
Cohagen, Montana

1 cup butter *or* margarine, softened
1/2 cup sugar
1/2 cup packed brown sugar
1 egg
3 teaspoons vanilla extract
1 teaspoon coconut extract
1-1/2 cups quick-cooking oats
1-1/4 cups all-purpose flour
1 teaspoon salt
1 teaspoon baking soda
1 cup flaked coconut, toasted
6 squares (1 ounce *each*) white baking chocolate, cut into 1-inch chunks
Additional sugar

In a mixing bowl, cream the butter and sugars. Add the egg and extracts; mix well. Combine the oats, flour, salt and baking soda; gradually add to creamed mixture. Stir in the coconut and chocolate.

Drop by tablespoonfuls 3 in. apart onto ungreased baking sheets. Flatten with a glass dipped in sugar. Bake at 350° for 9-11 minutes or until golden brown. Cool for 1 minute before removing to wire racks. **Yield:** about 5 dozen.

German Chocolate Cookies

(Pictured at right)

A handy boxed cake mix hurries along the preparation of these chewy cookies studded with chips and raisins. I make them for our family reunion each year, and they always get rave reviews.
—Leslie Henke
Louisville, Colorado

  1 package (18-1/4 ounces) German chocolate
     cake mix
  2 eggs
1/2 cup butter *or* margarine, melted
1/2 cup quick-cooking oats
  1 cup (6 ounces) semisweet chocolate chips
1/2 cup raisins

In a mixing bowl, combine dry cake mix, eggs, butter and oats; mix well. Stir in the chocolate chips and raisins. Drop by heaping tablespoonfuls 2 in. apart onto ungreased baking sheets. Bake at 350° for 9-11 minutes or until set. Cool for 5 minutes; remove to wire racks. **Yield:** about 3-1/2 dozen.

Chocolate Chip Butter Cookies

(Pictured below)

At the downtown Chicago law firm where I work, we often bring in goodies for special occasions. When co-workers hear I've baked these melt-in-your-mouth cookies, they make a special trip to my floor to sample them. Best of all, these crisp, buttery treats can be made in no time.
—Janis Gruca, Mokena, Illinois

  1 cup butter (no substitutes)
1/2 teaspoon vanilla extract
  2 cups all-purpose flour
  1 cup confectioners' sugar
  1 cup (6 ounces) miniature semisweet
     chocolate chips

Melt butter in a microwave oven or double boiler; stir in vanilla. Cool completely. In a large bowl, combine flour and sugar; stir in butter mixture and chocolate chips (mixture will be crumbly). Shape into 1-in. balls. Place 2 in. apart on ungreased baking sheets; flatten slightly. Bake at 375° for 12 minutes or until edges begin to brown. Cool on wire racks. **Yield:** about 4 dozen.

Chocolate Waffle Cookies

(Pictured on page 16)

I've had this recipe for years. It's economical to make, yet results in a delicious cookie. At Christmastime, I invite my grandchildren to join me—it makes a simple baking experience for them. They especially like sprinkling the powdered sugar on top...and the taste-testing afterward!
—Pat Oviatt, Zimmerman, Minnesota

1/4 cup butter (no substitutes), softened
  6 tablespoons sugar
  1 egg
1/2 teaspoon vanilla extract
  1 square (1 ounce) unsweetened chocolate,
     melted
1/2 cup all-purpose flour
Confectioners' sugar

In a mixing bowl, cream butter and sugar; beat in egg and vanilla until light and fluffy. Blend in chocolate. Add flour; mix well. Drop by rounded teaspoonfuls 1 in. apart onto a preheated waffle iron. Bake for 1 minute. Remove to a wire rack to cool. Dust with confectioners' sugar. **Yield:** about 1-1/2 dozen.

Crackle Cookies

(Pictured at right)

This cookie recipe comes close to the wonderful taste of chocolate that Mama was able to produce in her cakes and cookies. Because of the "crackles" in these cookies, my granddaughter tells me I've made a mistake when I bake them. "But they taste so good," she adds. —Ruth Cain
Hartselle, Alabama

- 1/2 cup sugar
- 1 egg
- 2 tablespoons vegetable oil
- 1 square (1 ounce) unsweetened chocolate, melted and cooled
- 1/2 teaspoon vanilla extract
- 1/2 cup all-purpose flour
- 1/2 to 3/4 teaspoon baking powder
- 1/8 teaspoon salt
- Confectioners' sugar

In a mixing bowl, combine sugar, egg, oil, chocolate and vanilla; mix well. Combine flour, baking powder and salt; gradually add to creamed mixture and mix well. Chill dough for at least 2 hours. With sugared hands, shape dough into 1-in. balls. Roll in confectioners' sugar. Place 2 in. apart on greased baking sheets. Bake at 350° for 10-12 minutes or until set. Remove to a wire rack to cool. **Yield:** about 1-1/2 dozen.

Chocolate Shortbread

(Pictured below)

This recipe has been in my files for a long time…probably from when I first learned to bake. Any chocolate lover will like these melt-in-your-mouth cookies.
—Sarah Bueckert, Austin, Manitoba

- 1/4 cup butter (no substitutes), softened
- 1/4 teaspoon vanilla extract
- 1/2 cup all-purpose flour
- 1/4 cup confectioners' sugar
- 1 to 2 tablespoons baking cocoa

In a mixing bowl, cream the butter. Add vanilla and mix well. Combine flour, sugar and cocoa; add to creamed mixture. Beat until dough holds together, about 3 minutes. Pat into a 9-in. x 4-in. rectangle. Cut into 2-in. x 1-1/2-in. strips. Place 1 in. apart on ungreased baking sheets. Prick with a fork. Bake at 300° for 20-25 minutes or until set. Cool for 5 minutes; remove to a wire rack to cool completely. **Yield:** 1 dozen.

Oat-Rageous Chocolate Chip Cookies

(Pictured on page 16)

My aunt gave me this recipe, and my family thinks these cookies are delicious. We enjoy all different kinds of cookies, and with this recipe, we can combine three of our favorite kinds—oatmeal, peanut butter and chocolate chip—in one! —Jaymie Noble, Kalamazoo, Michigan

- 1/2 cup butter *or* margarine, softened
- 1/2 cup creamy peanut butter
- 1/2 cup sugar
- 1/3 cup packed brown sugar
- 1 egg
- 1/2 teaspoon vanilla extract
- 1 cup all-purpose flour
- 1/2 cup quick-cooking oats
- 1 teaspoon baking soda
- 1/4 teaspoon salt
- 1 cup (6 ounces) semisweet chocolate chips

In a mixing bowl, cream butter, peanut butter and sugars; beat in egg and vanilla. Combine the flour, oats, baking soda and salt. Add to the creamed mixture and mix well. Stir in the chocolate chips. Drop by rounded teaspoonfuls onto ungreased baking sheets. Bake at 350° for 10-12 minutes or until lightly browned. Remove to a wire rack to cool. **Yield:** about 3 dozen.

Chocolate Nut Cookies

(Pictured above)

Folks are quick to grab one of these cookies when they see they're chocolate. Once they discover the nuts and vanilla chips, they grab a second and sometimes a third. I brought the recipe with me from my home in Kentucky.
—*Farralee Baldwin, Tucson, Arizona*

      1 cup butter *or* margarine, softened
  3/4 cup packed brown sugar
  1/2 cup sugar
      1 egg
      1 teaspoon almond extract
      2 cups all-purpose flour
  1/4 cup baking cocoa
      1 teaspoon baking soda
  1/2 teaspoon salt
      1 cup (6 ounces) vanilla *or* white chips
      1 cup chopped almonds

In a mixing bowl, cream butter and sugars. Add egg and extract; mix well. Combine the flour, cocoa, baking soda and salt; add to creamed mixture and mix well. Stir in the chips and nuts. Drop by teaspoonfuls onto ungreased baking sheets. Bake at 375° for 7-9 minutes. Cool on pans for 1 minute before removing to wire racks; cool completely. **Yield:** about 5 dozen.

Chocolate Marshmallow Cookies

(Pictured on page 16)

What fun! These double-chocolaty delights have a surprise inside. Atop the chocolate cookie base, marshmallow peeks out under chocolate icing. Kids love them.
—*June Formanek, Belle Plaine, Iowa*

  1/2 cup butter *or* margarine, softened
      1 cup sugar
      1 egg
  1/4 cup milk
      1 teaspoon vanilla extract
1-3/4 cups all-purpose flour
  1/3 cup baking cocoa
  1/2 teaspoon baking soda
  1/2 teaspoon salt

    16 to 18 large marshmallows
ICING:
      6 tablespoons butter *or* margarine
      2 tablespoons baking cocoa
  1/4 cup milk
1-3/4 cups confectioners' sugar
  1/2 teaspoon vanilla extract
Pecan halves

In a mixing bowl, cream butter and sugar. Add egg, milk and vanilla; mix well. Combine flour, cocoa, baking soda and salt; beat into creamed mixture. Drop by rounded teaspoonfuls onto ungreased baking sheets. Bake at 350° for 8 minutes. Meanwhile, cut marshmallows in half. Press a marshmallow half, cut side down, onto each cookie. Return to the oven for 2 minutes. Cool completely on a wire rack.

For icing, combine butter, cocoa and milk in a saucepan. Bring to a boil; boil for 1 minute, stirring constantly. Cool slightly; transfer to a small mixing bowl. Add confectioners' sugar and vanilla; beat well. Spread over the cooled cookies. Top each with a pecan half. **Yield:** about 3 dozen.

Old-Fashioned Whoopie Pies

(Pictured below)

Who can resist soft chocolate sandwich cookies filled with a layer of fluffy white frosting? Mom has made these for years...they're a treat that never lasted very long with me and my two brothers around. —*Maria Costello Monroe, North Carolina*

  1/2 cup baking cocoa
  1/2 cup hot water
  1/2 cup shortening
1-1/2 cups sugar
      2 eggs
      1 teaspoon vanilla extract
2-2/3 cups all-purpose flour
      1 teaspoon baking powder

1 teaspoon baking soda
1/4 teaspoon salt
1/2 cup buttermilk
FILLING:
3 tablespoons all-purpose flour
Dash salt
1 cup milk
3/4 cup shortening
1-1/2 cups confectioners' sugar
2 teaspoons vanilla extract

In a bowl, combine cocoa and water; mix well. Cool for 5 minutes. In a mixing bowl, cream shortening and sugar. Add cocoa mixture, eggs and vanilla; mix well. Combine dry ingredients. Add to creamed mixture alternately with buttermilk; mix well. Drop by rounded tablespoonfuls 2 in. apart onto greased baking sheets. Flatten slightly with a spoon. Bake at 350° for 10-12 minutes or until firm to the touch. Remove to wire racks to cool.

In a saucepan, combine flour and salt. Gradually whisk in milk until smooth; cook and stir over medium-high heat until thick, 5-7 minutes. Remove from heat. Cover and refrigerate until completely cool. In a mixing bowl, cream shortening, sugar and vanilla. Add chilled milk mixture; beat for 7 minutes or until fluffy. Spread filling on half of the cookies; top with remaining cookies. Store in the refrigerator. **Yield:** 2 dozen.

Chocolate Sandwich Cookies

(Pictured below)

These are my family's favorite cookies. They're soft, chewy and totally delicious. —Karen Bourne, Magrath, Alberta

2 packages (18-1/4 ounces *each*) devil's
   food cake mix
4 eggs, lightly beaten
2/3 cup vegetable oil
1 package (8 ounces) cream cheese, softened
1/2 cup butter *or* margarine, softened
3 to 4 cups confectioners' sugar
1/2 teaspoon vanilla extract
Red *and/or* green food coloring, optional

In a mixing bowl, beat cake mixes, eggs and oil (batter will be very stiff). Roll into 1-in. balls; place on ungreased baking sheets and flatten slightly. Bake at 350° for 8-10 minutes or until a slight indentation remains when lightly touched. Cool. In another mixing bowl, beat cream cheese and butter. Add sugar and vanilla; mix until smooth. If desired, tint with food coloring. Spread on bottom of half of the cookies. Top with remaining cookies. **Yield:** 4 dozen.

Pinwheel Cookies

(Pictured above)

These pretty pinwheel cookies have tempting swirly layers of orange and chocolate. —Paulette Morgan
Moorhead, Minnesota

1 cup butter (no substitutes), softened
1 package (3 ounces) cream cheese, softened
1 cup sugar
1 egg
1 tablespoon grated orange peel
1 teaspoon vanilla extract
3-1/2 cups all-purpose flour
1 teaspoon salt
FILLING:
1 cup (6 ounces) semisweet chocolate chips
1 package (3 ounces) cream cheese, softened
1/2 cup confectioners' sugar
1/4 cup orange juice

In a mixing bowl, cream butter, cream cheese and sugar. Add egg, orange peel and vanilla; mix well. Combine flour and salt; add to creamed mixture and mix well. Cover and chill for 4 hours or until firm. Meanwhile, combine all filling ingredients in a small saucepan. Cook and stir over low heat until smooth; set aside to cool.

On a floured surface, divide dough in half; roll each half into a 12-in. x 10-in. rectangle. Spread with filling. Carefully roll up into a tight jelly roll and wrap in waxed paper. Chill overnight. Remove waxed paper; cut rolls into 1/4-in. slices. Place on ungreased baking sheets. Bake at 375° for 8-10 minutes or until lightly browned. Remove to wire racks to cool. **Yield:** about 8 dozen.

Surprise Package Cookies

(Pictured at right)

Each of these buttery cookies has a chocolate mint candy inside. They're my very favorite cookie and are always part of our Christmas cookie trays. —Loraine Meyer
Bend, Oregon

> 1 cup butter (no substitutes), softened
> 1 cup sugar
> 1/2 cup packed brown sugar
> 2 eggs
> 1 teaspoon vanilla extract
> 3 cups all-purpose flour
> 1 teaspoon baking powder
> 1/2 teaspoon salt
> 65 mint Andes candies

In a mixing bowl, cream butter and sugars. Add eggs, one at a time, beating well after each addition. Beat in vanilla. Combine the flour, baking powder and salt; gradually add to creamed mixture. Cover and refrigerate for 2 hours or until easy to handle. With floured hands, shape a tablespoonful of dough around 42 candies, forming rectangular cookies.

Place 2 in. apart on greased baking sheets. Bake at 375° for 10-12 minutes or until edges are golden brown. Remove to wire racks to cool. In a microwave oven or saucepan, melt the remaining candies; drizzle over cookies. **Yield:** 3-1/2 dozen.

Chocolate Pretzel Cookies

(Pictured below)

These pretzel-shaped buttery chocolate cookies are covered in a rich mocha glaze and drizzled with white chocolate. They're beautiful to serve and give as gifts.
—Priscilla Anderson, Salt Lake City, Utah

> 1/2 cup butter (no substitutes), softened
> 2/3 cup sugar

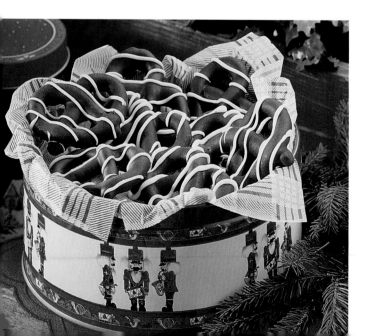

> 1 egg
> 2 squares (1 ounce *each*) unsweetened chocolate, melted and cooled
> 2 teaspoons vanilla extract
> 1-3/4 cups all-purpose flour
> 1/2 teaspoon salt
> MOCHA GLAZE:
> 1 cup (6 ounces) semisweet chocolate chips
> 1 teaspoon corn syrup
> 1 teaspoon shortening
> 1 cup confectioners' sugar
> 4 to 5 tablespoons hot coffee
> 2 squares (1 ounce *each*) white baking chocolate, melted

In a mixing bowl, cream butter and sugar. Add egg, chocolate and vanilla; mix well. Combine flour and salt; gradually add to creamed mixture and mix well. Cover and chill for 1 hour or until firm. Divide dough into fourths; form each portion into a 6-in. log. Divide each log into 12 pieces; roll each piece into a 9-in. rope. Place ropes on greased baking sheets; form into pretzel shapes and space 2 in. apart. Bake at 400° for 5-7 minutes or until firm. Cool 1 minute before removing to wire racks.

For glaze, heat the chocolate chips, corn syrup and shortening in a small saucepan over low heat until melted. Stir in sugar and enough coffee to make a smooth glaze. Dip pretzels; place on waxed paper or wire racks to harden. Drizzle with white chocolate; let stand until chocolate is completely set. Store in an airtight container. **Yield:** 4 dozen.

Holiday Hideaways

(Pictured at right)

People eagerly anticipate these tasty cookies as part of our "season's eatings" each year. The surprise cherry center surrounded by a fluffy cookie makes this treat especially fun. With the chocolate coating, they're almost like candy— and always the first to go! —Marianne Blazowich
Jeannette, Pennsylvania

3/4 cup sugar
2/3 cup butter-flavored shortening
1 egg
1 tablespoon milk
1 teaspoon vanilla extract
1-3/4 cups all-purpose flour
1 teaspoon baking powder
1/2 teaspoon baking soda
1/2 teaspoon salt
2 jars (10 ounces *each*) maraschino cherries, well drained
10 ounces white candy coating, *divided*
4 tablespoons butter-flavored shortening, *divided*
8 ounces dark chocolate candy coating
Finely chopped pecans

In a mixing bowl, cream sugar and shortening. Add egg, milk and vanilla. Combine dry ingredients; gradually add to the creamed mixture and mix well. Form 2 teaspoonfuls of dough into a ball. Flatten ball and place a cherry in the center; roll dough around cherry. Repeat with remaining dough and cherries.

Place balls 2 in. apart on ungreased baking sheets. Bake at 350° for 10-12 minutes or until set and the edges are lightly browned. Cool 1 minute before removing to wire racks to cool completely.

Grate 2 oz. white candy coating; set aside. Melt remaining white coating with 2 tablespoons shortening; melt dark coating with remaining shortening. Dip half the cookies into white coating; place on waxed paper. Sprinkle with pecans.

Dip the remaining cookies in dark coating; place on waxed paper. Sprinkle with grated white coating. Store in a covered container in the refrigerator. **Yield:** about 4-1/2 dozen.

Chocolate Mint Wafers

(Pictured above)

These festive cookies remind my family of after-dinner mints. With my husband and our two children munching on these chocolaty treats with cool mint filling, a batch never stays around long. —Annette Esau
Durham, Ontario

2/3 cup butter *or* margarine, softened
1/2 cup sugar
1/2 cup packed brown sugar
1/4 cup milk
1 egg
2 cups all-purpose flour
3/4 cup baking cocoa
1 teaspoon baking powder
1/2 teaspoon baking soda
1/4 teaspoon salt
FILLING:
2-3/4 cups confectioners' sugar
1/4 cup half-and-half cream
1/4 teaspoon peppermint extract
1/4 teaspoon salt
Green food coloring

In a mixing bowl, cream butter and sugars. Add milk and egg; mix well. Combine dry ingredients; gradually add to creamed mixture and mix well. Cover and chill 2 hours or until firm. Roll chilled dough on a floured surface to 1/8-in. thickness. Cut with a 1-1/2-in. cookie cutter and place 1 in. apart on greased baking sheets.

Bake at 375° for 5-6 minutes or until edges are lightly browned. Remove to wire racks to cool completely. Combine filling ingredients; spread on half of the cookies and top with another cookie. **Yield:** about 7-1/2 dozen.

Chocolate Truffle Cookies

(Pictured above)

Here's a snack for serious chocolate lovers. These enticing cookies are crisp on the outside and soft on the inside, somewhat bittersweet and very chocolaty. I usually make them to share at get-togethers...otherwise, I'd eat them all myself! I'm always asked for the recipe.
—Delaine Fortenberry, McComb, Mississippi

 4 squares (1 ounce *each*) unsweetened chocolate
 2 cups (12 ounces) semisweet chocolate
 chips, *divided*
 1/3 cup butter (no substitutes)
 1 cup sugar
 3 eggs
1-1/2 teaspoons vanilla extract
 1/2 cup all-purpose flour
 2 tablespoons baking cocoa
 1/4 teaspoon baking powder
 1/4 teaspoon salt
Confectioners' sugar

In a microwave oven or double boiler, melt unsweetened chocolate, 1 cup of chocolate chips and butter; cool for 10 minutes. In a mixing bowl, beat sugar and eggs for 2 minutes. Beat in vanilla and chocolate mixture. Combine flour, cocoa, baking powder and salt; beat into chocolate mixture. Stir in remaining chocolate chips.

Cover and chill for at least 3 hours. Remove about 1 cup of dough. With lightly floured hands, roll into 1-in. balls. Place on ungreased baking sheets. Bake at 350° for 10-12 minutes or until lightly puffed and set. Cool on pan 3-4 minutes before removing to a wire rack to cool completely. Repeat with remaining dough. Dust with confectioners' sugar. **Yield:** about 4 dozen.

Triple Chocolate Kisses

(Pictured at right)

These crisp meringue cookies with a chocolate center are easy to make but look like you spent a lot of time. When our son and daughter-in-law moved into their first home on Valentine's Day, I prepared them a nice dinner and gave them a batch of these treats. —Evelyn Lindburg
Shenandoah, Iowa

 2 egg whites
 1/4 teaspoon cream of tartar
 1/2 cup sugar
 1/4 teaspoon almond extract
 1 square (1 ounce) semisweet chocolate, grated
 42 milk chocolate kisses
Baking cocoa

In a mixing bowl, beat egg whites until foamy. Add cream of tartar; beat until soft peaks form, about 6 minutes. Gradually add sugar, beating until stiff peaks form, about 6 minutes. Beat in extract. Fold in grated chocolate.

Insert a medium open-star tip in a pastry or plastic bag. Fill with the meringue. On lightly greased baking sheets, pipe forty-two 1-in. circles. Press a chocolate kiss into the center of each. Pipe meringue around each kiss in continuous circles from the base to the top until kiss is completely covered. Dust with cocoa. Bake at 325° for 15-18 minutes or until the edges are lightly browned. Immediately remove to wire racks to cool. **Yield:** 3-1/2 dozen.

Chewy Brownie Cookies

Biting into these tempting cookies reveals they're like chewy brownies inside. —Jonie Adams, Albion, Michigan

 2/3 cup shortening
1-1/2 cups packed brown sugar
 1 tablespoon water
 1 teaspoon vanilla extract
 2 eggs
1-1/2 cups all-purpose flour
 1/3 cup baking cocoa
 1/2 teaspoon salt
 1/4 teaspoon baking soda
 2 cups (12 ounces) semisweet chocolate chips
 1/2 cup chopped walnuts *or* pecans, optional

In a large mixing bowl, cream shortening, sugar, water and vanilla. Beat in the eggs. Combine flour, cocoa, salt

and baking soda; gradually add to creamed mixture and beat just until blended. Stir in chocolate chips and nuts if desired. Drop by rounded teaspoonfuls 2 in. apart on ungreased baking sheets. Bake at 375° for 7-9 minutes. Cool for 2 minutes before removing to wire racks. **Yield:** 3 dozen.

Chocolate Peanut Butter Cookies

(Pictured below)

Sandwich cookies are always a hit, and homemade ones like these that feature peanut butter and chocolate are guaranteed to please! Whenever we visit friends, they ask if we'll bring a batch of these cookies.
—Vickie Rhoads, Eugene, Oregon

      2 cups butter *or* margarine
  1/4 cup shortening
      2 cups baking cocoa
      1 cup chocolate syrup
  1/2 cup peanut butter
      6 eggs
      5 cups sugar
      5 teaspoons vanilla extract
      5 cups all-purpose flour
      3 teaspoons baking soda
      1 teaspoon salt
FILLING:
  1/2 cup butter *or* margarine, softened
      1 cup chunky peanut butter
      1 cup milk
      2 teaspoons vanilla extract
    11 cups confectioners' sugar

In a saucepan over low heat, melt butter and shortening. Remove from the heat; stir in cocoa, chocolate syrup and peanut butter until smooth. Cool.

In a large mixing bowl, beat eggs and sugar until lemon-colored. Beat in the chocolate mixture and vanilla. Combine the flour, baking soda and salt; gradually add to creamed mixture. Drop by teaspoonfuls 2 in. apart

onto ungreased baking sheets. Flatten with a glass dipped in sugar. Bake at 350° for 10-12 minutes or until surface cracks. Cool for 2 minutes before removing to wire racks.

In a mixing bowl, beat butter and peanut butter. Beat in milk and vanilla. Gradually add confectioners' sugar, beating until blended. Spread on the bottom of half of the cookies; top with remaining cookies. **Yield:** 11 dozen.

Monster Chip Cookies

(Pictured above)

I share these treats with "monsters" who ring my doorbell on Halloween. I also give them as Christmas gifts.
—Judy Mabrey, Myrtle Beach, South Carolina

      1 cup shortening
  1/2 cup butter *or* margarine, softened
  1-1/3 cups sugar
      1 cup packed brown sugar
      4 eggs
      3 teaspoons vanilla extract
      1 teaspoon lemon juice
      3 cups all-purpose flour
  1/2 cup quick-cooking oats
      2 teaspoons baking soda
  1-1/2 teaspoons salt
      1 teaspoon ground cinnamon
      4 cups (24 ounces) semisweet chocolate chips
      2 cups chopped nuts

In a mixing bowl, cream shortening, butter and sugars until light and fluffy, about 5 minutes. Add eggs, one at a time, beating well after each. Add vanilla and lemon juice. Combine the dry ingredients; add to creamed mixture and mix well. Stir in chips and nuts. Refrigerate 8 hours or overnight.

Drop by 1/4 cupfuls 3 in. apart onto lightly greased baking sheets. Bake at 350° for 14-16 minutes or until lightly browned and center is set. Cool for 2 minutes before removing to wire racks. **Yield:** about 3 dozen.

Mom's Chocolate Chip Cookies

My mom always brightened my lunch with these yummy cookies when I was growing up. —Tammy Orr
Wharton, New Jersey

    1 cup butter *or* margarine, softened
  3/4 cup packed brown sugar
  1/4 cup sugar
    1 package (3.4 ounces) instant vanilla
      pudding mix
    2 eggs, lightly beaten
    1 teaspoon vanilla extract
2-1/4 cups all-purpose flour
    1 teaspoon baking soda
    2 cups (12 ounces) semisweet chocolate chips

In a mixing bowl, cream butter and sugars. Add pudding mix, eggs and vanilla. Combine flour and baking soda; add to creamed mixture and mix well. Fold in chocolate chips. Drop by teaspoonfuls onto ungreased baking sheets. Bake at 375° for 10-12 minutes or until lightly browned. Remove to wire racks to cool. **Yield:** 4 dozen.

Chocolate Malted Cookies

(Pictured below)

These cookies are the next best thing to a good old-fashioned malted milk. With malted milk powder, chocolate syrup plus chocolate chips and chunks, these are the best cookies I've ever tasted...and with six kids, I've made a lot of cookies over the years. —Teri Rasey-Bolf
Cadillac, Michigan

    1 cup butter-flavored shortening
1-1/4 cups packed brown sugar
  1/2 cup malted milk powder
    2 tablespoons chocolate syrup
    1 tablespoon vanilla extract
    1 egg
    2 cups all-purpose flour
    1 teaspoon baking soda
  1/2 teaspoon salt

1-1/2 cups semisweet chocolate chunks
    1 cup milk chocolate chips

In a mixing bowl, combine the first five ingredients; beat for 2 minutes. Add egg. Combine the flour, baking soda and salt; gradually add to creamed mixture, mixing well after each addition. Stir in chocolate chunks and chips. Shape into 2-in. balls; place 3 in. apart on ungreased baking sheets. Bake at 375° for 12-14 minutes or until golden brown. Cool for 2 minutes before removing to a wire rack. **Yield:** about 1-1/2 dozen.

Chocolate Macadamia Nut Cookies

I've been hosting an annual Christmas cookie exhcange for over 35 years now. Each guest brings 6 dozen cookies to share. This recipe is always a favorite. —Arliene Hillinger
Rancho Palos Verdes, California

  10 tablespoons butter (no substitutes), softened
  3/4 cup packed brown sugar
    1 teaspoon vanilla extract
    1 egg, lightly beaten
    1 cup all-purpose flour
  3/4 teaspoon baking powder
  1/8 teaspoon baking soda
  1/8 teaspoon salt
1-1/2 cups semisweet chocolate chips
  3/4 cup coarsely chopped macadamia nuts
  3/4 cup coarsely chopped pecans
CARAMEL GLAZE:
  12 caramels, unwrapped
    2 tablespoons whipping cream

In a mixing bowl, cream butter, sugar and vanilla. Add egg. Combine flour, baking powder, baking soda and salt; add to creamed mixture and mix well. Fold in chocolate chips and nuts. Drop by teaspoonfuls 2 in. apart onto greased baking sheets. Bake at 350° for 10-12 minutes or until golden. Cool on a wire rack.

For glaze, melt the caramels and cream in a saucepan over low heat, stirring until smooth. Drizzle over cooled cookies. **Yield:** 2 dozen.

Chocolaty Double Crunchers

(Pictured above)

I first tried these fun crispy cookies at a family picnic when I was a child. Packed with oats, cornflakes and coconut, they quickly became a "regular" at our house. Years later, I still make them for my own family. —Cheryl Johnson
Upper Marlboro, Maryland

1/2 cup butter *or* margarine, softened
1/2 cup sugar
1/2 cup packed brown sugar
1 egg
1/2 teaspoon vanilla extract
1 cup all-purpose flour
1/2 teaspoon baking soda
1/4 teaspoon salt
1 cup quick-cooking oats
1 cup crushed cornflakes
1/2 cup flaked coconut
FILLING:
2 packages (3 ounces *each*) cream cheese, softened
1-1/2 cups confectioners' sugar
2 cups (12 ounces) semisweet chocolate chips, melted

In a mixing bowl, cream butter and sugars. Add egg and vanilla; mix well. Combine flour, baking soda and salt; add to creamed mixture and mix well. Add oats, cornflakes and coconut. Shape into 1-in. balls and place 2 in. apart on greased baking sheets. Flatten with a glass dipped lightly in flour. Bake at 350° for 8-10 minutes or until lightly browned. Remove to wire racks to cool.

For filling, beat cream cheese and sugar until smooth. Add the chocolate; mix well. Spread about 1 tablespoon on half of the cookies and top each with another cookie. Store in the refrigerator. **Yield:** about 2 dozen.

Chocolate Thumbprints

(Pictured below)

A group of friends had a weekly "movie night" during winters on Martha's Vineyard, and we'd take turns making a chocolate treat to share. These terrific cookies were an instant success. —Laura Bryant German
West Warren, Massachusetts

1/2 cup butter *or* margarine, softened
2/3 cup sugar
1 egg, *separated*
2 tablespoons milk
1 teaspoon vanilla extract
1 cup all-purpose flour
1/3 cup baking cocoa
1/4 teaspoon salt
1 cup finely chopped walnuts
FILLING:
1/2 cup confectioners' sugar
1 tablespoon butter *or* margarine, softened
2 teaspoons milk
1/4 teaspoon vanilla extract
26 milk chocolate kisses, unwrapped

In a mixing bowl, beat butter, sugar, egg yolk, milk and vanilla until light and fluffy. Combine flour, cocoa and salt; gradually add to creamed mixture. Cover and chill 1 hour or until firm enough to roll into balls. Meanwhile, in a small bowl, lightly beat egg white. Shape dough into 1-in. balls; dip in egg white, then roll in nuts. Place on greased baking sheets. Make an indentation with thumb in center of each cookie. Bake at 350° for 10-12 minutes or until center is set.

Combine the first four filling ingredients in a small bowl; mix until smooth. Spoon 1/4 teaspoon into each warm cookie; gently press a chocolate kiss in the center. Carefully remove from baking sheet to wire racks to cool. **Yield:** about 2 dozen.

BLACK FOREST BROWNIES, PAGE 34

TRIPLE FUDGE BROWNIES,
PAGE 43

COCONUT CHIP NUT BARS,
PAGE 32

FUDGY NUT BROWNIES, PAGE 36

Bars & Brownies

Holiday Brownies

(Pictured above)

Folks always ask for this recipe whenever I make these brownies. I make batches and batches of this tasty treat before the holidays and give them as gifts. —Erna Madsen Bothell, Washington

1/2 **cup butter (no substitutes)**
    4 **squares (1 ounce** *each***) unsweetened chocolate**
    2 **cups sugar**
1-1/4 **cups all-purpose flour**
    2 **teaspoons ground cinnamon**
1/2 **teaspoon salt**
    4 **eggs, beaten**
    1 **teaspoon vanilla extract**
1-1/2 **cups halved red** *and/or* **green candied cherries, divided**
    1 **cup chopped walnuts**

In a heavy saucepan, melt butter and chocolate over low heat. Cool for 10 minutes. In a bowl, combine the sugar, flour, cinnamon and salt. Stir in the cooled chocolate mixture, eggs and vanilla until smooth. Fold in 1-1/4 cups cherries and the walnuts. Transfer to a greased 13-in. x 9-in. x 2-in. baking pan. Arrange remaining cherries over top. Bake at 350° for 35 minutes or until a toothpick inserted near the center comes out clean. Cool on a wire rack. Cut into bars. **Yield:** 2 dozen.

Coconut Chip Nut Bars

(Pictured on page 30)

There's something for everyone in these delectable bars, from coconut and chocolate chips to walnuts and toffee. They're popular with kids and adults alike—so make a big batch. You'll be amazed at how fast they vanish!
    —Judith Strohmeyer, Albrightsville, Pennsylvania

1-3/4 **cups all-purpose flour**
    3/4 **cup confectioners' sugar**
    1/4 **cup baking cocoa**
1-1/4 **cups cold butter** *or* **margarine**
    1 **can (14 ounces) sweetened condensed milk**

    2 **cups (12 ounces) semisweet chocolate chips,** *divided*
    1 **teaspoon vanilla extract**
    1 **cup chopped walnuts**
1/2 **cup flaked coconut**
1/2 **cup English toffee bits** *or* **almond brickle chips**

In a bowl, combine the flour, sugar and cocoa. Cut in butter until mixture resembles coarse crumbs. Press firmly into a greased 13-in. x 9-in. x 2-in. baking pan. Bake at 350° for 10 minutes.

Meanwhile, in a saucepan, combine milk and 1 cup chocolate chips; cook and stir over low heat until smooth and chips are melted. Stir in vanilla. Pour over crust. Sprinkle with walnuts and remaining chocolate chips. Top with coconut and toffee bits. Gently press down into chocolate layer. Bake at 350° for 18-20 minutes or until firm. Cool on a wire rack. Cut into bars. **Yield:** 3 dozen.

Really Rocky Road Brownies

(Pictured below)

This rich fudgy dessert recipe is from a family reunion cookbook that I compiled. My niece, Olivia Fallon, contributed the recipe.   —Brenda Wood, Egbert, Ontario

1-1/2 **cups butter (no substitutes)**
    8 **squares (1 ounce** *each***) unsweetened chocolate**
    6 **eggs**
    3 **cups sugar**
    1 **tablespoon vanilla extract**
1-1/2 **cups all-purpose flour**
    1 **cup chopped walnuts, optional**
TOPPING:
    2 **cups miniature marshmallows**
    1 **square (1 ounce) unsweetened chocolate, melted**

In a heavy saucepan, melt butter and chocolate over medium heat; cool slightly. In a mixing bowl, beat eggs for 2 minutes. Gradually add sugar; beat until thick, about 3 minutes. Stir in chocolate mixture and vanilla. Fold in flour and nuts if desired.

Pour into two greased and floured 9-in. square baking pans. Bake at 350° for 25-30 minutes or until a toothpick inserted near the center comes out with moist crumbs (do not overbake). Sprinkle each pan with 1 cup of marshmallows. Broil until marshmallows are golden brown, about 30-60 seconds. Drizzle with chocolate. **Yield:** 4 dozen.

Moist Cake Brownies

(Pictured above)

These brownies have been in my recipe collection since I was 9 years old. I've added to and altered the recipe over the years, and now I think it has the perfect amount of everything, including semisweet and milk chocolate chips and pecans. —Louise Stacey, Dane, Wisconsin

2/3 cup butter *or* margarine
3/4 cup baking cocoa
1/4 cup vegetable oil
2 cups sugar
4 eggs
2 teaspoons vanilla extract
1-1/2 cups all-purpose flour
1 teaspoon baking powder
1 teaspoon salt
2/3 cup semisweet chocolate chips
1/2 cup milk chocolate chips
1 cup coarsely chopped pecans
Confectioners' sugar
Pecan halves, toasted, optional

Melt butter in a large saucepan. Whisk in cocoa and oil until smooth. Cook and stir over low heat until cocoa is blended. Remove from the heat; stir in sugar. Add eggs, one at a time, stirring well after each addition. Stir in vanilla.

Combine flour, baking powder and salt; add to cocoa mixture. Stir in chocolate chips and nuts. Spread into a greased 13-in. x 9-in. x 2-in. baking pan. Bake at 350° for 25-30 minutes or until a toothpick inserted near the center comes out clean. Cool. Dust with confectioners' sugar. Garnish with pecan halves if desired. **Yield:** 2 dozen.

Chocolate Cheese Layered Bars

(Pictured below)

These rich and chocolaty bars are a hit at church and family gatherings. Folks love the chocolate and cream cheese layers. —Sharon Schaa, Murray, Iowa

1/2 cup butter (no substitutes), softened
1 cup sugar
2 eggs
1 square (1 ounce) unsweetened chocolate, melted
1 teaspoon vanilla extract
1 cup all-purpose flour
1 teaspoon baking powder
1/2 cup chopped pecans
CHEESE LAYER:
6 ounces cream cheese, softened
1/4 cup butter, softened
1/2 cup sugar
1 egg
2 tablespoons all-purpose flour
1/2 teaspoon vanilla extract
1/4 cup chopped pecans
1 cup (6 ounces) semisweet chocolate chips
3 cups miniature marshmallows
TOPPING:
1/4 cup butter
2 ounces cream cheese, softened
1 square (1 ounce) unsweetened chocolate
2 tablespoons milk
3 cups confectioners' sugar
1 teaspoon vanilla extract

In a mixing bowl, cream butter and sugar. Add eggs, chocolate and vanilla; mix well. Combine flour and baking powder; stir into chocolate mixture. Fold in pecans. Pour into a greased 13-in. x 9-in. x 2-in. baking pan.

In a mixing bowl, combine cream cheese and butter. Beat in the sugar, egg, flour and vanilla; mix well. Fold in pecans. Spread over the chocolate layer; sprinkle with chips. Bake at 350° for 20-25 minutes or until edges pull away from sides of pan. Sprinkle with marshmallows; bake 2 minutes longer or until puffed. Spread evenly over cream cheese layer. Cool on a wire rack.

In a saucepan, combine first four topping ingredients. Cook and stir over low heat until smooth. Transfer to a mixing bowl. Add the confectioners' sugar and vanilla; beat until smooth. Spread over cooled bars. Store in the refrigerator. **Yield:** 2 dozen.

Chocolate Raspberry Bars

(Pictured at right)

My family loves these rich, sweet bars. The chocolate and raspberry jam go together so well. I make a lot of cookies and bars, but these special treats are my favorite. They're so pretty served on a platter.
—Kathy Smedstad
Silverton, Oregon

 1 cup all-purpose flour
 1/4 cup confectioners' sugar
 1/2 cup butter *or* margarine
FILLING:
 1/2 cup seedless raspberry jam
 4 ounces cream cheese, softened
 2 tablespoons milk
 1 cup (6 ounces) vanilla *or* white chips, melted
GLAZE:
 3/4 cup semisweet chocolate chips
 2 tablespoons shortening

In a bowl, combine flour and confectioners' sugar; cut in butter until crumbly. Press into an ungreased 9-in. square baking pan. Bake at 375° for 15-18 minutes or until browned. Spread jam over warm crust.

In a small mixing bowl, beat cream cheese and milk until smooth. Add vanilla chips; beat until smooth. Spread carefully over jam layer. Cool completely. Chill until set, about 1 hour. For glaze, melt chocolate chips and shortening; spread over filling. Chill for 10 minutes. Cut into bars; chill another hour. Store in the refrigerator. **Yield:** 3 dozen.

Chocolate Peanut Butter Brownies

(Pictured below)

My husband and I have two sons, both away at college. I send these brownies to them regularly, and they tell me that they have to hide a few from their roommates just so they can make sure there will be some left! —Patsy Burgin
Lebanon, Indiana

 2 squares (1 ounce *each*) unsweetened chocolate
 1/2 cup butter (no substitutes)

 2 eggs
 1 cup sugar
 1/2 cup all-purpose flour
FILLING:
 1-1/2 cups confectioners' sugar
 1/2 cup creamy peanut butter
 1/4 cup butter, softened
 2 to 3 tablespoons half-and-half cream *or* milk
GLAZE:
 1 square (1 ounce) semisweet baking chocolate
 1 tablespoon butter

In a small saucepan, melt chocolate and butter over low heat; set aside. In a mixing bowl, beat eggs and sugar until light and pale-colored. Add flour and melted chocolate; stir well. Pour into a greased 9-in. square baking pan. Bake at 350° for 25 minutes or until a toothpick inserted near the center comes out clean. Cool.

For filling, beat confectioners' sugar, peanut butter and butter in a mixing bowl. Stir in cream until mixture reaches desired spreading consistency. Spread over cooled brownies; cover and chill until firm.

For glaze, melt chocolate and butter in a saucepan, stirring until smooth. Drizzle over the filling. Chill before cutting. Store in the refrigerator. **Yield:** about 5 dozen.

Black Forest Brownies

(Pictured on page 30)

These brownies are easy to make, and the ingredients are always on hand. Even my boyfriend, who doesn't like most sweets, can't pass up these brownies.   —Toni Reeves
Medicine Hat, Alberta

1-1/3 cups all-purpose flour
 1 teaspoon baking powder
 1/2 teaspoon salt
 1 cup butter *or* margarine
 1 cup baking cocoa
 4 eggs, beaten
 2 cups sugar
1-1/2 teaspoons vanilla extract
 1 teaspoon almond extract
 1 cup chopped maraschino cherries
 1/2 cup chopped nuts

ICING:

- 1/4 cup butter *or* margarine, softened
- 1 teaspoon vanilla extract
- 2 cups confectioners' sugar
- 6 tablespoons baking cocoa
- 1/4 cup milk
- 1/4 cup chopped nuts

Combine flour, baking powder and salt; set aside. In a large saucepan, melt butter. Remove from the heat and stir in cocoa until smooth. Blend in eggs, sugar and extracts. Stir in flour mixture, cherries and nuts. Pour into a greased 13-in. x 9-in. x 2-in. baking pan. Bake at 350° for 35 minutes or until a toothpick inserted near the center comes out clean.

For icing, blend butter, vanilla, sugar, cocoa and milk until smooth; spread over warm brownies. Sprinkle with nuts. Cool. **Yield:** 3 dozen.

German Chocolate Brownies

(Pictured below)

Even as a young girl, I was always going through recipe books in search of something new to make. That's how I came across these brownies. I bring them to family reunions and church dinners—but they're great anytime!
—*Karen Grimes, Stephens City, Virginia*

- 1/2 cup butter (no substitutes)
- 1 package (4 ounces) German sweet chocolate, broken into squares
- 1/2 cup sugar
- 1 teaspoon vanilla extract
- 2 eggs, lightly beaten
- 1 cup all-purpose flour
- 1/2 teaspoon baking powder
- 1/4 teaspoon salt

TOPPING:

- 2 tablespoons butter, melted
- 1/2 cup packed brown sugar
- 1 cup flaked coconut
- 1/2 cup chopped pecans
- 2 tablespoons corn syrup
- 2 tablespoons milk

In a saucepan, melt butter and chocolate, stirring until smooth. Cool slightly. Add sugar and vanilla; mix. Beat in the eggs. Mix in flour, baking powder and salt. Pour into a greased 9-in. square baking pan. Bake at 350° for 18-22 minutes or until a toothpick inserted near the center comes out clean.

For topping, combine butter and brown sugar in a bowl. Add coconut, pecans, corn syrup and milk; mix well. Drop by teaspoonfuls onto warm brownies; spread evenly. Broil several inches from the heat for 2-4 minutes or until top is browned and bubbly. **Yield:** 16 brownies.

Apricot Angel Brownies

(Pictured above)

To tell the truth, I'm not a chocoholic. I enjoy fruit desserts and custards more than anything. So my brownies have neither milk nor dark chocolate—but still satisfy every sweet tooth. —*Tamara Sellman, Barrington, Illinois*

- 4 squares (1 ounce *each*) white baking chocolate
- 1/3 cup butter (no substitutes)
- 1/2 cup packed brown sugar
- 2 eggs, beaten
- 1/4 teaspoon vanilla extract
- 3/4 cup all-purpose flour
- 1/2 teaspoon baking powder
- 1/4 teaspoon salt
- 1 cup finely chopped dried apricots
- 1/4 cup sliced almonds
- 1/4 cup flaked coconut

In a saucepan, melt chocolate and butter over low heat, stirring constantly until all of the chocolate is melted. Remove from the heat; stir in brown sugar, eggs and vanilla until blended. Set aside. In a bowl, combine flour, baking powder and salt. Stir in chocolate mixture. Combine apricots, almonds and coconut; stir half into the batter. Pour into a greased 9-in. square baking pan. Sprinkle remaining apricot mixture on top. Bake at 350° for 25 minutes or until golden brown. Cool. **Yield:** about 2 dozen.

Out-of-This-World Brownies

(Pictured above)

For company and every time there is a local bake sale, I bake a batch of these fabulous brownies. Most everyone who tastes them says, "Yum! These are the best brownies I have ever eaten!" —Jeannette Haley, Council, Idaho

- 1 cup butter (no substitutes), softened
- 2 cups sugar
- 4 eggs
- 2 teaspoons vanilla extract
- 2 cups all-purpose flour
- 1/4 cup plus 3 tablespoons baking cocoa
- 1/8 teaspoon salt
BROWN BUTTER FROSTING:
- 1/2 cup butter
- 4 cups confectioners' sugar
- 1/4 cup plus 2 teaspoons half-and-half cream
- 2 teaspoons vanilla extract
GLAZE:
- 1 square (1 ounce) unsweetened chocolate
- 1 tablespoon butter

In a mixing bowl, cream butter and sugar. Add the eggs, one at a time, beating well after each addition. Beat in vanilla. Combine flour, cocoa and salt; gradually add to the creamed mixture. Spread into an ungreased 13-in. x 9-in. x 2-in. baking pan. Bake at 350° for 25-30 minutes or until a toothpick inserted near the center comes out clean (do not overbake). Cool on wire rack.

For frosting, in a heavy saucepan, cook and stir butter over medium heat for 5-7 minutes or until golden brown. Pour into a mixing bowl; beat in the confectioners' sugar, cream and vanilla. Frost cooled brownies. For glaze, melt chocolate and butter; drizzle over the frosting. Cut into bars. **Yield:** 3 dozen.

Fudgy Nut Brownies

(Pictured on page 30)

This recipe came from an old roommate, who is now a grandmother. While in our early 20s, we never imagined we'd be sharing brownie recipes after all these years.
—Ruth Sparer Stern, Shadow Hills, California

- 2-1/2 cups semisweet chocolate chips
- 1 cup butter *or* margarine
- 1 cup sugar
- 1/4 teaspoon salt
- 4 eggs, lightly beaten
- 2 teaspoons vanilla extract
- 3/4 cup all-purpose flour
- 1 cup coarsely chopped hazelnuts *or* almonds, toasted
TOPPING:
- 12 squares (1 ounce *each*) semisweet chocolate
- 1 tablespoon shortening
- 3 squares (1 ounce *each*) white baking chocolate

In a saucepan over low heat, melt chocolate chips and butter; remove from the heat. Add sugar and salt; stir until dissolved. Cool for 10 minutes. Stir in eggs, vanilla, flour and nuts. Spread into a greased 15-in. x 10-in. x 1-in. baking pan. Bake at 350° for 25-30 minutes or until a toothpick inserted near the center comes out with moist crumbs (do not overbake). Cool on a wire rack.

For topping, in a heavy saucepan or microwave oven, heat semisweet chocolate and shortening just until melted. Spread over brownies. Melt white chocolate. Pour into a small heavy-duty resealable plastic bag; cut a small hole in corner of bag. Pipe thin lines 1 in. apart widthwise. Beginning about 1 in. from a wide side, gently pull a toothpick through the lines to the opposite side. Wipe toothpick clean. Then pull toothpick through lines in opposite direction. Repeat over entire top at 1-in. intervals. Cut into bars. **Yield:** about 2-1/2 dozen.

Super Brownies

(Pictured below)

Even though he's not a chocolate fan, my husband likes these brownies. I fix them for family, company and potlucks.

They're so popular, in fact, I've even entered them at the state fair.
—Bernice Muilenburg, Molalla, Oregon

1/2 cup butter *or* margarine
1-1/2 cups sugar
4-2/3 cups semisweet chocolate chips, *divided*
3 tablespoons hot water
4 eggs
5 teaspoons vanilla extract
1-1/2 cups all-purpose flour
1/2 teaspoon baking soda
1/2 teaspoon salt
2 cups coarsely chopped macadamia nuts *or* pecans, *divided*

In a saucepan over medium heat, melt butter and sugar. Remove from the heat; stir in 2 cups chocolate chips until melted. Pour into a mixing bowl; beat in water. Add eggs, one at a time, beating well after each addition. Add vanilla. Combine flour, baking soda and salt; beat into the chocolate mixture until smooth. Stir in 2 cups of chocolate chips and 1 cup of nuts. Pour into a greased 13-in. x 9-in. x 2-in. baking pan. Sprinkle with remaining chips and nuts. Bake at 325° for 55 minutes or until the center is set (do not overbake). **Yield:** about 3-1/2 dozen.

Double-Decker Brownies

(Pictured above right)

Family and friends are in for a treat when they bite into these doubly delicious brownies. Luscious layers of chocolate and butterscotch are topped off with a creamy frosting.
—Heather Hooker, Belmont, Ontario

CHOCOLATE LAYER:
2 eggs, lightly beaten
1 cup sugar
3/4 cup all-purpose flour
1/2 cup chopped walnuts
Pinch salt
1/2 cup butter *or* margarine, melted
1/4 cup baking cocoa
BUTTERSCOTCH LAYER:
1/2 cup butter *or* margarine, softened
1-1/2 cups packed brown sugar
2 eggs
2 teaspoons vanilla extract
1-1/2 cups all-purpose flour
1/4 teaspoon salt
1/2 cup chopped walnuts
FROSTING:
1/2 cup packed brown sugar
1/4 cup butter *or* margarine
3 tablespoons milk
1-1/2 cups confectioners' sugar
1/3 cup semisweet chocolate chips
1/3 cup butterscotch chips
1 tablespoon shortening

In a bowl, combine eggs, sugar, flour, walnuts and salt. In another bowl, stir butter and cocoa until smooth; add to egg mixture and blend well with a wooden spoon. Pour into a greased 13-in. x 9-in. x 2-in. baking pan; set aside.

For butterscotch layer, cream butter and brown sugar in a mixing bowl. Beat in eggs and vanilla. Stir in flour, salt and walnuts. Spoon over the chocolate layer. Bake at 350° for 30-35 minutes or until brownies begin to pull away from sides of pan; cool.

For frosting, combine brown sugar, butter and milk in a small saucepan; bring to a boil and boil for 2 minutes. Remove from the heat; stir in confectioners' sugar until smooth. Quickly spread over brownies. In a small saucepan over low heat, melt chocolate chips, butterscotch chips and shortening, stirring frequently. Drizzle over frosting. **Yield:** 3 dozen.

Brownie Toppings

WHEN your favorite brownie recipe calls for chocolate chips or nuts to be stirred into the batter or sprinkled over the top before baking, try using other flavored chips or varying the nuts for a different taste.

For kids who don't care for nuts, try adding crisp rice cereal to chocolate frosting instead.

Topping brownie batter with seasonal colored M&M's (red and green for Christmas, pastels for Easter, etc.) is a simple way to make your brownies special for holidays throughout the year.

Chocolate Maple Bars

(Pictured below)

My family runs a maple syrup operation, and I'm always looking for new ways to incorporate maple syrup into my cooking and baking. These bars are delicious!
—Cathy Schumacher, Alto, Michigan

  1/2 cup shortening
  3/4 cup maple syrup
  1/2 cup sugar
    3 eggs
    3 tablespoons milk
    1 teaspoon vanilla extract
1-1/4 cups all-purpose flour
  1/4 teaspoon baking powder
  1/4 teaspoon salt
1-1/2 squares (1-1/2 ounces) unsweetened chocolate, melted
  1/2 cup chopped pecans
  1/2 cup flaked coconut
FROSTING:
  1/4 cup butter *or* margarine, softened
    1 cup confectioners' sugar
  1/2 cup baking cocoa
  1/2 cup maple syrup
    1 cup miniature marshmallows

In a mixing bowl, cream the shortening, syrup and sugar. Beat in the eggs, milk and vanilla. Combine the flour, baking powder and salt; add to creamed mixture and mix well. Remove half of the batter to another bowl.

Combine melted chocolate and pecans; stir into one bowl. Spread into a greased 13-in. x 9-in. x 2-in. baking pan. Add coconut to remaining batter. Spread carefully over chocolate batter. Bake at 350° for 25 minutes or until a toothpick inserted near the center comes out clean. Cool completely on a wire rack.

For frosting, in a small mixing bowl, cream butter. Gradually add confectioners' sugar and cocoa. Slowly add syrup, beating until smooth. Fold in marshmallows. Frost bars. **Yield:** 3 dozen.

Chocolate Chip Meringue Bars

(Pictured above)

My husband and I are sugar beet farmers. I've made these bars many times for my family, and we all love them.
—Elaine Swenson, Kindred, North Dakota

    1 cup shortening
1-1/2 cups packed brown sugar, *divided*
  1/2 cup sugar
    3 eggs, *separated*
    1 tablespoon cold water
    1 tablespoon vanilla extract
    2 cups all-purpose flour
    1 teaspoon baking soda
  1/8 teaspoon salt
    1 cup (6 ounces) semisweet chocolate chips
    1 cup ground salted peanuts

In a mixing bowl, cream shortening, 1/2 cup of brown sugar and sugar. Add egg yolks; mix well. Combine the water and vanilla. Combine flour, baking soda and salt; add to creamed mixture alternately with water mixture. Mix well. Spread into a greased 15-in. x 10-in. x 1-in. baking pan. Sprinkle with chocolate chips.

In a small mixing bowl, beat egg whites until soft peaks form. Add the remaining brown sugar, 2 tablespoons at a time, beating well after each addition. Beat until stiff peaks form. Spread over chocolate chips. Top with peanuts. Bake at 350° for 30-35 minutes. **Yield:** about 3 dozen.

Chocolate Caramel Bars

Taking dessert or another treat to a church or school potluck is never a problem for me. I jump at the chance to offer these rich, chocolaty bars.
—Steve Mirro
Cape Coral, Florida

1 package (14 ounces) caramels
1 can (5 ounces) evaporated milk,
   divided
3/4 cup butter *or* margarine, softened
1 package (18-1/4 ounces) German
   chocolate cake mix
2 cups (12 ounces) semisweet
   chocolate chips

In a small saucepan over low heat, melt caramels with 1/3 cup milk. Meanwhile, in a mixing bowl, cream butter. Add cake mix and remaining milk; mix well. Spread half of the dough into a greased 13-in. x 9-in. x 2-in. baking pan. Bake at 350° for 6 minutes; sprinkle chocolate chips over dough. Gently spread caramel mixture over chips. Drop remaining dough by tablespoonfuls over caramel layer. Return to the oven for 15 minutes. **Yield:** 3 dozen.

Chocolate Cherry Bars

(Pictured below)

These tempting bars are simple to make with cherry pie filling, crunchy almonds and chocolate chips. I took them to a church supper and everyone wanted the recipe. Some people said the sweet treats reminded them of chocolate-covered cherries. —Tina Dierking, Canaan, Maine

1-3/4 cups all-purpose flour
   1 cup sugar
1/4 cup baking cocoa
   1 cup cold butter *or* margarine
   1 egg, lightly beaten
   1 teaspoon almond extract
   1 can (21 ounces) cherry pie filling
   2 cups (12 ounces) semisweet chocolate chips
   1 cup chopped almonds

In a bowl, combine the flour, sugar and cocoa. Cut in butter until crumbly. Add egg and almond extract until blended; set aside 1 cup for topping. Press remaining crumb mixture into a greased 13-in. x 9-in. x 2-in. baking pan. Carefully top with pie filling. Combine chocolate chips, almonds and reserved crumb mixture; sprinkle over pie filling. Bake at 350° for 35-40 minutes or until a toothpick inserted near the center comes out clean. Cool; refrigerate for at least 2 hours before cutting. **Yield:** 3 dozen.

Black-Bottom Banana Bars

(Pictured above)

These bars stay very moist, and their rich banana and chocolate flavor is even better the second day. My mother-in-law gave me this recipe, and it's a big favorite with both my husband and two sons. —Renee Wright, Ferryville, Wisconsin

1/2 cup butter *or* margarine, softened
   1 cup sugar
   1 egg
   1 teaspoon vanilla extract
1-1/2 cups mashed ripe bananas (about 3 medium)
1-1/2 cups all-purpose flour
   1 teaspoon baking powder
   1 teaspoon baking soda
1/2 teaspoon salt
1/4 cup baking cocoa

In a mixing bowl, cream butter and sugar. Add egg and vanilla; beat until thoroughly combined. Blend in the bananas. Combine the flour, baking powder, baking soda and salt; add to creamed mixture and mix well.

Divide the batter in half. Add cocoa to one half; spread into a greased 13-in. x 9-in. x 2-in. baking pan. Spoon the remaining batter on top and swirl with a knife. Bake at 350° for 25 minutes or until a toothpick inserted near the center comes out clean. Cool. **Yield:** 2-1/2 to 3 dozen.

Peanut Butter Caramel Bars

(Pictured above)

When my husband, Bob, and our three sons sit down to dinner, they ask, "What's for dessert?" I have a happy group of guys when I report that these rich bars are on the menu.   —Lee Ann Karnowski, Stevens Point, Wisconsin

    1 package (18-1/4 ounces) yellow cake mix
1/2 cup butter *or* margarine, softened
    1 egg
  20 miniature peanut butter cups, chopped
    2 tablespoons cornstarch
    1 jar (12-1/4 ounces) caramel ice cream topping
1/4 cup peanut butter
1/2 cup salted peanuts
TOPPING:
    1 can (16 ounces) milk chocolate frosting
1/2 cup chopped salted peanuts

In a mixing bowl, combine the dry cake mix, butter and egg; beat until no longer crumbly, about 3 minutes. Stir in the peanut butter cups. Press into a greased 13-in. x 9-in. x 2-in. baking pan. Bake at 350° for 18-22 minutes or until lightly browned.

Meanwhile, in a saucepan, combine cornstarch, caramel topping and peanut butter until smooth. Cook over low heat, stirring occasionally, until mixture comes to a boil, about 25 minutes. Cook and stir 1-2 minutes longer. Remove from the heat; stir in peanuts. Spread evenly over warm crust.

Bake 6-7 minutes longer or until almost set. Cool completely on a wire rack. Spread with frosting; sprinkle with peanuts. Refrigerate for at least 1 hour before cutting. Store in the refrigerator. **Yield:** about 3 dozen.

Fudge-Nut Oatmeal Bars

When I make these bars for lunches and snacks, they're gone in a jiffy!   —Kim Stoller, Smithville, Ohio

    1 cup butter *or* margarine, softened
    2 cups packed brown sugar
    2 eggs
    2 teaspoons vanilla extract
    3 cups quick-cooking oats
2-1/2 cups all-purpose flour
    1 teaspoon baking soda
    1 teaspoon salt
FUDGE FILLING:
    1 can (14 ounces) sweetened condensed milk
    2 cups (12 ounces) semisweet chocolate chips
    2 tablespoons butter *or* margarine
1/2 teaspoon salt
    2 teaspoons vanilla extract
    1 cup chopped walnuts

In a mixing bowl, cream butter and brown sugar. Add eggs and vanilla; mix well. Combine oats, flour, baking soda and salt; add to the creamed mixture. Spread two-thirds in the bottom of an ungreased 15-in. x 10-in. x 1-in. baking pan; set aside.

For filling, heat milk, chocolate chips, butter and salt in a saucepan or microwave-safe bowl until melted. Remove from the heat; stir in vanilla and walnuts. Spread over oat mixture in pan. Drop remaining oat mixture by tablespoonfuls over chocolate. Bake at 350° for 20-25 minutes. **Yield:** 2-1/2 to 3 dozen.

Polka-Dot Cookie Bars

(Pictured below)

To serve a group, these lightly sweet bars are a lot easier to make than fussing with individual cookies. They're my favorite.   —Elizabeth Poire, Kailua-Kona, Hawaii

    1 cup butter *or* margarine, softened
3/4 cup sugar
3/4 cup packed brown sugar
    2 eggs
1/2 teaspoon almond extract
2-1/4 cups all-purpose flour
1/3 cup baking cocoa

1 teaspoon baking soda
1/2 teaspoon salt
1 package (10 to 12 ounces) vanilla *or* white
chips, *divided*

In a mixing bowl, cream butter and sugars. Add eggs, one at a time, beating well after each addition. Beat in extract. Combine flour, cocoa, baking soda and salt; gradually add to the creamed mixture.

Set aside 1/4 cup vanilla chips; stir remaining chips into batter. Spread in a greased 15-in. x 10-in. x 1-in. baking pan. Sprinkle with reserved chips. Bake at 375° for 18-23 minutes or until a toothpick inserted near the center comes out clean. Cool before cutting. **Yield:** 4 dozen.

Chocolate Dipped Brownies

(Pictured above right)

My family calls these bars "the world's chocolatiest brownies" and is more than happy to gobble up a batch whenever I make them. —Jackie Archer, Clinton, Iowa

 3/4 cup sugar
 1/3 cup butter *or* margarine
 2 tablespoons water
 4 cups (24 ounces) semisweet chocolate
 chips, *divided*
 1 teaspoon vanilla extract
 2 eggs
 3/4 cup all-purpose flour
 1/2 teaspoon salt
 1/4 teaspoon baking soda
 2 tablespoons shortening
 1/2 cup chopped pecans, toasted

In a saucepan over medium heat, bring sugar, butter and water to a boil; remove from the heat. Stir in 1 cup of chocolate chips and vanilla; stir until smooth. Cool for 5 minutes. Beat in eggs, one at a time, until well mixed.

Combine flour, salt and baking soda; stir into chocolate mixture. Stir in another cup of chips. Pour into a greased 9-in. square baking pan. Bake at 325° for 35 minutes. Cool completely.

Place in the freezer for 30-40 minutes (do not freeze completely). Cut into bars. In a microwave or double boiler, melt remaining chips with shortening; stir until smooth. Using a small fork, dip brownies to completely coat; shake off excess. Place on waxed paper-lined baking sheets; immediately sprinkle with nuts. Allow to harden. Store in an airtight container in a cool place. **Yield:** 3 dozen.

Chocolate Date Squares

(Pictured below left)

My mother-in-law used to send batches of these moist bars to my husband when he was in the Army. They've become a favorite with our family. —Pat Walter
Pine Island, Minnesota

 2 cups chopped dates
 1 cup hot water
 1 cup sugar
 2/3 cup shortening
 2 eggs
1-1/2 cups all-purpose flour
 1 teaspoon baking soda
 1/2 teaspoon salt
TOPPING:
 1 cup (6 ounces) semisweet chocolate chips
 1/2 cup packed brown sugar
 1/2 cup chopped nuts

In a bowl, combine dates and water; set aside to cool (do not drain). In a mixing bowl, cream sugar and shortening. Add eggs, flour, baking soda and salt; mix well. Add dates. Pour into a greased and floured 13-in. x 9-in. x 2-in. baking pan. Combine the topping ingredients; sprinkle over batter. Bake at 350° for 40 minutes or until a toothpick inserted in the center comes out clean. **Yield:** 24 servings.

Two-Tone Fudge Brownies

(Pictured below)

These moist fudgy brownies have a scrumptious topping that tastes just like chocolate chip cookie dough! My husband and I and our young sons enjoy church fellowship at frequent potluck meals. Everyone loves these brownies…and they make enough to feed a crowd.

—Rebecca Kays, Klamath Falls, Oregon

- 1 cup (6 ounces) semisweet chocolate chips
- 1/2 cup butter *or* margarine, softened
- 1 cup sugar
- 3 eggs
- 1 teaspoon vanilla extract
- 1-1/4 cups all-purpose flour
- 1/4 teaspoon baking soda
- 3/4 cup chopped walnuts

COOKIE DOUGH LAYER:
- 1/2 cup butter *or* margarine, softened
- 1/2 cup packed brown sugar
- 1/4 cup sugar
- 3 tablespoons milk
- 1 teaspoon vanilla extract
- 1 cup all-purpose flour
- 1 cup (6 ounces) semisweet chocolate chips

In a microwave-safe bowl, melt chocolate chips. Cool slightly. In a mixing bowl, cream butter and sugar. Add eggs and vanilla; mix well. Stir in melted chocolate. Combine flour and baking soda; add to batter. Stir in the walnuts.

Spread into a greased 13-in. x 9-in. x 2-in. baking pan. Bake at 350° for 16-22 minutes or until a toothpick inserted near the center comes out clean. Cool on a wire rack.

In a mixing bowl, cream butter and sugars. Beat in milk and vanilla. Gradually add flour. Stir in chocolate chips. Drop by tablespoonfuls over cooled brownies; carefully spread over top. Cut into squares. Store in the refrigerator. **Yield:** 4 dozen.

Editor's Note: Cookie dough layer is not baked and does not contain eggs.

Chocolate Walnut Squares

(Pictured above)

Rich and satisfying, these bars create a symphony of flavors with every bite. The nutty crust, exquisite chocolate layer and creamy frosting make this dessert one of my personal favorites. It's fun to take these treats to a potluck.

—Anne Heinonen, Howell, Michigan

- 1 cup butter *or* margarine, softened
- 2 cups sugar
- 4 eggs, lightly beaten
- 1 tablespoon vanilla extract
- 2 cups all-purpose flour
- 1/2 teaspoon salt
- 2 cups chopped walnuts
- 2 squares (1 ounce *each*) unsweetened chocolate, melted

FROSTING:
- 5 tablespoons all-purpose flour
- 1 cup milk
- 1 cup butter *or* margarine, softened
- 1 cup confectioners' sugar
- 2 teaspoons vanilla extract

In a mixing bowl, cream butter and sugar. Beat in eggs and vanilla. Add flour and salt; mix well. Fold in walnuts. Spread half of the batter into a greased 13-in. x 9-in. x 2-in. baking pan. Add chocolate to the remaining batter; mix well. Carefully spread over batter in pan. Bake at 350° for 30-35 minutes or until a toothpick inserted near the center comes out clean. Cool completely.

For frosting, mix flour and milk in a saucepan. Cook and stir over medium heat until a thick paste forms, about 10 minutes. Cool completely. In a mixing bowl, cream butter and confectioners' sugar. Add vanilla and mix well. Gradually add the milk mixture; beat for 5 minutes. Frost. Store in the refrigerator. **Yield:** 20-24 servings.

Swiss Chocolate Brownies

(Pictured above)

When our two grown children were at home, I baked these brownies often. These days, I make them for special occasions—everyone thinks they're quite nice.
—Gloria Stange, Claresholm, Alberta

- 1 cup water
- 1/2 cup butter (no substitutes)
- 1-1/2 squares (1-1/2 ounces) unsweetened chocolate
- 2 cups all-purpose flour
- 2 cups sugar
- 1 teaspoon baking soda
- 1/2 teaspoon salt
- 2 eggs, lightly beaten
- 1/2 cup sour cream
- 1/2 teaspoon vanilla extract
- 1 cup chopped walnuts

ICING:
- 1/2 cup butter
- 1-1/2 squares (1-1/2 ounces) unsweetened chocolate
- 3 cups confectioners' sugar, *divided*
- 5 tablespoons milk
- 1 teaspoon vanilla extract

In a saucepan, bring water, butter and chocolate to a boil. Boil for 1 minute. Remove from the heat; cool. In a mixing bowl, combine flour, sugar, baking soda and salt. Add chocolate mixture and mix. Add eggs, sour cream and vanilla; mix. Fold in walnuts. Pour into a greased 15-in. x 10-in. x 1-in. baking pan. Bake at 350° for 20-25 minutes or until a toothpick inserted near the center comes out clean. Cool for 10 minutes.

For icing, melt butter and chocolate. Place in a mixing bowl; mix in 1-1/2 cups confectioners' sugar. Add milk, vanilla and remaining sugar; beat until smooth. Spread over warm brownies. **Yield:** about 3 dozen.

Triple Fudge Brownies

(Pictured on page 30)

When you're in a hurry to make dessert, here's a "mix of mixes" that's so convenient and quick. The result is a big pan of very rich, fudgy brownies. —*Denise Nebel*
Wayland, Iowa

- 1 package (3.9 ounces) instant chocolate pudding mix
- 1 package (18-1/4 ounces) chocolate cake mix
- 2 cups (12 ounces) semisweet chocolate chips
- Confectioners' sugar

Prepare pudding according to package directions. Whisk in cake mix. Stir in chocolate chips. Pour into a greased 15-in. x 10-in. x 1-in. baking pan. Bake at 350° for 30-35 minutes or until the top springs back when lightly touched. Dust with confectioners' sugar. **Yield:** 4 dozen.

Marble Squares

(Pictured below)

With cream cheese, sour cream and lots of chocolate, these bars are simply scrumptious. I'm sure you'll agree.
—Pat Habiger, Spearville, Kansas

- 1 package (8 ounces) cream cheese, softened
- 2-1/3 cups sugar, *divided*
- 3 eggs
- 3/4 cup water
- 1/2 cup butter (no substitutes)
- 1-1/2 squares (1-1/2 ounces) unsweetened chocolate
- 2 cups all-purpose flour
- 1/2 cup sour cream
- 1 teaspoon baking soda
- 1/2 teaspoon salt
- 1 cup (6 ounces) semisweet chocolate chips

In a mixing bowl, beat cream cheese and 1/3 cup sugar until light and fluffy. Beat in 1 egg; set aside. In a saucepan, bring water, butter and chocolate to a boil, stirring occasionally. Remove from the heat. Mix in flour and remaining sugar. Stir in sour cream, baking soda, salt and remaining eggs until smooth.

Pour into a greased and floured 15-in. x 10-in. x 1-in. baking pan. Dollop cream cheese mixture over the top; cut through batter to create a marbled effect. Sprinkle with chocolate chips. Bake at 375° for 30-35 minutes or until a toothpick comes out clean. Cool. **Yield:** about 5 dozen.

Chocolate Oat Squares

(Pictured above)

When you bring these to a gathering, guests will start at the dessert table! Chock-full of chocolate and walnuts, they will satisfy any sweet tooth. I often make a second batch just for my family. —Jennifer Eilts, Central City, Nebraska

1 cup plus 2 tablespoons butter *or* margarine, softened, *divided*
2 cups packed brown sugar
2 eggs
4 teaspoons vanilla extract, *divided*
3 cups quick-cooking oats
2-1/2 cups all-purpose flour
1-1/2 teaspoons salt, *divided*
1 teaspoon baking soda
1 can (14 ounces) sweetened condensed milk
2 cups (12 ounces) semisweet chocolate chips
1 cup chopped walnuts

In a mixing bowl, cream 1 cup butter and brown sugar. Beat in eggs and 2 teaspoons vanilla. Combine the oats, flour, 1 teaspoon salt and baking soda; stir into creamed mixture. Press two-thirds of oat mixture into a greased 15-in. x 10-in. x 1-in. baking pan.

In a saucepan, combine milk, chocolate chips and remaining butter and salt. Cook and stir over low heat until chocolate is melted. Remove from the heat; stir in walnuts and remaining vanilla. Spread over the crust. Sprinkle with remaining oat mixture. Bake at 350° for 25 minutes or until golden brown. Cool. Cut into squares. **Yield:** 4 dozen.

S'mores Crumb Bars

You don't have to be camping to enjoy the great taste of s'mores. Plus, since you can whip up a batch of these tempting bars in your kitchen, you don't have to put up with mosquitoes! —Darlene Markel, Sublimity, Oregon

3 cups graham cracker crumbs
3/4 cup butter *or* margarine, melted
1/3 cup sugar

3 cups miniature marshmallows
2 cups (12 ounces) semisweet chocolate chips

Combine the graham cracker crumbs, butter and sugar; press half into a greased 13-in. x 9-in. x 2-in. baking pan. Sprinkle with marshmallows and chocolate chips. Top with remaining crumb mixture; press firmly. Bake at 375° for 10 minutes. Remove from the oven and immediately press top firmly with spatula. Cool completely. Cut into bars. **Yield:** 3 dozen.

Cookie Dough Brownies

(Pictured below)

When I take these rich chocolaty brownies to any get-together, I carry along the recipe, too, because it always gets requested. Children of all ages love the tempting cookie dough filling. —Wendy Bailey, Elida, Ohio

2 cups sugar
1-1/2 cups all-purpose flour
1/2 cup baking cocoa
1/2 teaspoon salt
1 cup vegetable oil
4 eggs
2 teaspoons vanilla extract
1/2 cup chopped walnuts, optional
FILLING:
1/2 cup butter *or* margarine, softened
1/2 cup packed brown sugar
1/4 cup sugar
2 tablespoons milk
1 teaspoon vanilla extract
1 cup all-purpose flour
GLAZE:
1 cup (6 ounces) semisweet chocolate chips
1 tablespoon shortening
3/4 cup chopped walnuts

In a mixing bowl, combine sugar, flour, cocoa and salt. Add oil, eggs and vanilla; beat at medium speed for 3

minutes. Stir in walnuts if desired. Pour into a greased 13-in. x 9-in. x 2-in. baking pan. Bake at 350° for 30 minutes or until a toothpick inserted near the center comes out clean. Cool completely.

For filling, cream butter and sugars in a mixing bowl. Add milk and vanilla; mix well. Beat in flour. Spread over the brownies; chill until firm. For glaze, melt chocolate chips and shortening in a saucepan, stirring until smooth. Spread over filling. Immediately sprinkle with nuts, pressing down slightly. **Yield:** 3 dozen.

Chocolate Chip Graham Bars

(Pictured below)

These moist chewy bars are a satisfying snack any time of day. Packed with oats, chocolate chips, crunchy peanuts and graham cereal, they have something for everyone. —Sandi Michalski, Macy, Indiana

- 3/4 cup butter (no substitutes), softened
- 3/4 cup sugar
- 3/4 cup packed brown sugar
- 2 eggs
- 1 teaspoon vanilla extract
- 1-1/2 cups all-purpose flour
- 1-1/2 cups Golden Grahams cereal, crushed
- 3/4 cup plus 2 tablespoons quick-cooking oats, *divided*
- 1 teaspoon baking soda
- 1/2 teaspoon baking powder
- 1/2 teaspoon salt
- 1 cup salted peanuts, *divided*
- 1 cup (6 ounces) semisweet chocolate chips, *divided*

In a large mixing bowl, cream butter and sugars. Add eggs, one at a time, beating well after each addition. Beat in vanilla. Combine the flour, cereal, 3/4 cup oats, baking soda, baking powder and salt; gradually add to creamed mixture. Stir in 3/4 cup peanuts and 2/3 cup chocolate chips.

Spread into a greased 13-in. x 9-in. x 2-in. baking pan. Coarsely chop remaining peanuts; sprinkle over the top with remaining oats and chips. Bake at 350° for 25-30 minutes or until golden brown. Cool on a wire rack. Cut into bars. **Yield:** 2 dozen.

Cherry Cocoa Shortbread Squares

(Pictured above)

Whenever there is a potluck at work or a family gathering, I'm asked to bring these delectable bars. I found the recipe years ago and have made it countless times since. —Bettie Martin, Oneida, Wisconsin

- 1/2 cup plus 2 tablespoons butter (no substitutes), softened, *divided*
- 1/4 cup sugar
- 1 cup all-purpose flour
- 2 tablespoons baking cocoa
- 2 cups confectioners' sugar
- 2 tablespoons milk
- 1/2 teaspoon vanilla extract
- 18 maraschino cherries, halved

GLAZE:
- 1 square (1 ounce) unsweetened chocolate
- 1-1/2 teaspoons butter

In a mixing bowl, cream 1/2 cup butter and sugar. Beat in flour and cocoa (mixture will be crumbly). Spread into a greased 9-in. square baking pan. Bake at 350° for 15 minutes or until surface is set. Cool on a wire rack for 15 minutes.

Meanwhile, in a mixing bowl, combine confectioners' sugar and remaining butter; beat in milk and vanilla until smooth. Spread over crust. Pat cherries dry with a paper towel; arrange over frosting and press down gently.

In a microwave-safe bowl, melt the chocolate and butter; stir until smooth. Drizzle over cherries. Refrigerate until glaze has hardened. Cut into squares. **Yield:** 3 dozen.

Very Chocolate Brownies

(Pictured below)

I've spent years trying brownie recipes in search of the perfect one. This scrumptious version might be it. The fluffy top layer is absolutely heavenly. —Arlene Kay Butler
Ogden, Utah

- 4 squares (1 ounce *each*) unsweetened chocolate
- 3/4 cup butter (no substitutes)
- 2 cups sugar
- 3 eggs
- 1 teaspoon vanilla extract
- 1 cup all-purpose flour
- 1 cup coarsely chopped walnuts

TOPPING:
- 1 cup (6 ounces) semisweet chocolate chips
- 1/4 cup water
- 2 tablespoons butter
- 1 cup whipping cream, whipped

In a microwave oven or double boiler, melt chocolate and butter; cool for 10 minutes. Add sugar; mix well. Stir in eggs and vanilla. Add flour; mix well. Stir in walnuts. Line a 13-in. x 9-in. x 2-in. baking pan with foil and grease the foil. Pour batter into pan. Bake at 350° for 25-30 minutes or until a toothpick inserted near the center comes out with moist crumbs (do not overbake). Cool completely.

For topping, melt chocolate chips, water and butter in a microwave oven or double boiler; stir until smooth. Cool to room temperature. Fold in whipped cream. Spread over brownies. Chill before cutting. Store leftovers in the refrigerator. **Yield:** 3 dozen.

Dark Chocolate Mocha Brownies

(Pictured above)

Dark chocolate is a favorite around our house, so these frosted brownies are a hit. I came up with this treat by reworking a recipe I've used for a long time. We have six children, and these brownies always disappear so fast.
—Linda McCoy, Oostburg, Wisconsin

- 2 cups packed brown sugar
- 1 cup butter *or* margarine, melted
- 3 eggs
- 1 tablespoon instant coffee granules
- 2 teaspoons vanilla extract
- 1 cup all-purpose flour
- 1 cup baking cocoa
- 1/2 teaspoon baking powder
- 1/2 teaspoon salt
- 6 squares (1 ounce *each*) bittersweet chocolate, coarsely chopped

FROSTING:
- 1/4 cup butter *or* margarine, melted
- 3 tablespoons sour cream
- 2 teaspoons vanilla extract
- 2-3/4 to 3 cups confectioners' sugar
- 2 squares (1 ounce *each*) bittersweet chocolate, grated

In a mixing bowl, combine brown sugar and butter. Beat in eggs, one at a time. Add coffee and vanilla; mix well. Combine the flour, cocoa, baking powder and salt; add to sugar mixture and mix well. Stir in chocolate. Spread into a greased 13-in. x 9-in. x 2-in. baking pan. Bake at 350° for 25-30 minutes or until a toothpick inserted near the center comes out clean. Cool on a wire rack.

For frosting, combine butter, sour cream and vanilla; mix well. Gradually stir in sugar until frosting is smooth and reaches desired consistency. Frost brownies. Sprinkle with grated chocolate. **Yield:** 5 dozen.

Cookies 'n' Cream Brownies

(Pictured below)

You won't want to frost these brownies, since the marbled top is too pretty to cover up. Besides, the tasty cream cheese layer makes them taste like they're already frosted. The crushed cookies add extra chocolate flavor and a fun crunch. —Darlene Markel, Sublimity, Oregon

CREAM CHEESE LAYER:
- 1 package (8 ounces) cream cheese, softened
- 1/4 cup sugar
- 1 egg
- 1/2 teaspoon vanilla extract

BROWNIE LAYER:
- 1/2 cup butter *or* margarine, melted
- 1/2 cup sugar
- 1/2 cup packed brown sugar
- 1/2 cup baking cocoa
- 2 eggs
- 1/2 cup all-purpose flour
- 1 teaspoon baking powder
- 1 teaspoon vanilla extract
- 12 cream-filled chocolate sandwich cookies, crushed

In a small mixing bowl, beat the cream cheese, sugar, egg and vanilla until smooth; set aside. For brownie layer, combine butter, sugars and cocoa in a large mixing bowl; blend well. Add eggs, one at a time, beating well after each addition. Combine flour and baking powder; stir into the cocoa mixture. Stir in vanilla and cookie crumbs.

Pour into a greased 11-in. x 7-in. x 2-in. baking pan. Spoon cream cheese mixture over batter; cut through batter with a knife to swirl. Bake at 350° for 25-30 minutes or until a toothpick inserted near the center comes out with moist crumbs. Cool completely. **Yield:** 2 dozen.

Chocolate Macaroon Brownies

(Pictured above and on front cover)

The brownie base makes this recipe different from other macaroon bars—in fact, that gives you a nice option if you don't have a lot of time. Just substitute a boxed brownie mix and top it with the filling and frosting. —Emily Engel Quill Lake, Saskatchewan

BROWNIE BASE:
- 1-1/2 cups sugar
- 2/3 cup vegetable oil
- 4 eggs, beaten
- 1 teaspoon vanilla extract
- 1-1/3 cups all-purpose flour
- 2/3 cup baking cocoa
- 1 teaspoon baking powder
- 1/2 teaspoon salt

COCONUT FILLING:
- 1 can (14 ounces) sweetened condensed milk
- 3 cups flaked coconut
- 1 teaspoon vanilla extract

BUTTER FROSTING:
- 2 cups confectioners' sugar
- 1/2 cup baking cocoa
- 1/2 cup butter *or* margarine, softened
- 1 teaspoon vanilla extract
- 1 to 2 tablespoons milk, *divided*

In a large mixing bowl, combine sugar and oil. Add eggs and vanilla; mix well. Combine dry ingredients; add to bowl and mix until smooth. Pour into a greased 13-in. x 9-in. x 2-in. baking pan. Combine all filling ingredients in a small bowl; spoon over brownie base. Bake at 350° for 30-35 minutes or until a toothpick inserted near the center comes out clean. Cool.

Meanwhile, for frosting, combine sugar, cocoa, butter, vanilla and 1 tablespoon milk in a small mixing bowl. Beat until fluffy. Add remaining milk if needed to achieve desired spreading consistency. Spread over filling. **Yield:** about 2 dozen.

DELUXE CHIP CHEESECAKE, PAGE 65

CHOCOLATE CHEESECAKE,
PAGE 62

CHOCOLATE STRAWBERRY TORTE,
PAGE 57

BROWNIE SWIRL CHEESECAKE, PAGE 63

Cakes & Cheesecakes

Chocolate Truffle Cheesecake

(Pictured above)

If you like to revel in chocolate, then this is the cheesecake for you. Every creamy bite melts in your mouth.
—Mary Jones, Cumberland, Maine

1-1/2 cups chocolate wafer crumbs
   2 tablespoons sugar
  1/4 cup butter *or* margarine, melted
FILLING:
  1/4 cup semisweet chocolate chips
  1/4 cup whipping cream
   3 packages (8 ounces *each*) cream cheese,
     softened
   1 cup sugar
  1/3 cup baking cocoa
   3 eggs
   1 teaspoon vanilla extract
TOPPING:
1-1/2 cups semisweet chocolate chips
  1/4 cup whipping cream
   1 teaspoon vanilla extract

In a small bowl, combine cookie crumbs and sugar; stir in butter. Press onto the bottom and 1-1/2 in. up the sides of a greased 9-in. springform pan. Place on a baking sheet. Bake at 350° for 10 minutes. Cool on a wire rack. Reduce heat to 325°.

In a saucepan over low heat, melt chocolate chips; stir until smooth. Remove from the heat; add cream and mix well. Set aside. In a mixing bowl, beat cream cheese and sugar until smooth. Add cocoa and beat well. Add eggs; beat on low just until combined. Stir in vanilla and reserved chocolate mixture just until blended. Pour over crust. Place pan on a baking sheet. Bake for 45-50 minutes or until center is almost set.

For topping, melt chocolate chips in a saucepan over low heat, stirring until smooth. Remove from the heat. Stir in cream and vanilla; mix well. Spread over filling. Refrigerate overnight. Carefully run a knife around edge of pan to loosen. Remove sides of pan. Just before serving, garnish with whipped cream and miniature chocolate kisses if desired. Refrigerate leftovers. **Yield:** 12 servings.

Triple Layer Brownie Cake

(Pictured below)

A little of this tall, rich brownie cake goes a long way, so you'll have plenty of pieces left to share. It's a sure way to satisfy true chocolate lovers and is perfect for any occasion. *—Barbara Dean, Littleton, Colorado*

1-1/2 cups butter (no substitutes)
   6 squares (1 ounce *each*) unsweetened chocolate
   3 cups sugar
   5 eggs
1-1/2 teaspoons vanilla extract
1-1/2 cups all-purpose flour
  3/4 teaspoon salt
FROSTING:
   2 packages (8 ounces *each*) semisweet baking
     chocolate
   3 cups whipping cream
  1/2 cup sugar, optional
   2 milk chocolate candy bars (1.55 ounces *each*),
     shaved

In a microwave oven or double boiler, melt butter and chocolate. Stir in sugar. Add eggs, one at a time, beating well after each. Stir in vanilla, flour and salt; mix well. Pour into three greased and floured 9-in. round baking pans. Bake at 350° for 23-25 minutes or until a toothpick inserted near the center comes out clean. Cool for 10 minutes; remove from pan to a wire rack to cool completely.

For frosting, melt chocolate in a heavy saucepan over medium heat. Gradually stir in cream and sugar if desired until well blended. Heat to a gentle boil; boil and stir for 1 minute. Remove from the heat; transfer to a mixing bowl. Refrigerate for 2-3 hours or until mixture reaches a pudding-like consistency, stirring a few times. Beat until soft peaks form. Immediately spread between layers and over top and sides of cake. Sprinkle with shaved chocolate. Store in the refrigerator. **Yield:** 16-20 servings.

Choco-Scotch Marble Cake

(Pictured above)

This recipe was given to me many years ago by a friend. Teaming chocolate with butterscotch for a marble cake makes it more flavorful and colorful than the usual chocolate-vanilla combination. This rich family favorite is very moist and keeps well. —Pam Giammattei Valatie, New York

      1 package (18-1/4 ounces) yellow cake mix
      1 package (3.4 ounces) instant butterscotch pudding mix
      4 eggs
      1 cup (8 ounces) sour cream
  1/3 cup vegetable oil
  1/2 cup butterscotch chips
      1 square (1 ounce) unsweetened chocolate, melted
FROSTING:
1-1/2 cups butterscotch chips, melted
      1 square (1 ounce) unsweetened chocolate, melted
      5 to 6 tablespoons half-and-half cream
      2 tablespoons finely chopped pecans

In a large mixing bowl, combine cake mix, pudding mix, eggs, sour cream and oil; beat on low speed for 2 minutes. Divide batter in half; stir butterscotch chips into half and chocolate into the other half. Spoon half of the butterscotch batter in a greased 10-in. fluted tube pan; top with half of the chocolate batter. Repeat layers. Cut through batter with a knife to swirl.

Bake at 350° for 40-45 minutes or until a toothpick inserted near the center comes out clean. Cool for 10 minutes before removing from pan to a wire rack to cool completely.

For frosting, combine butterscotch chips and chocolate in a small mixing bowl. Beat in enough cream until the frosting is smooth and reaches desired spreading consistency. Spread over top of cake. Sprinkle with pecans.
Yield: 12-16 servings.

Sour Cream Chocolate Cake

(Pictured below)

Impressive to look at but easy to make, this cake is a good old-fashioned "Sunday supper" dessert that is simply scrumptious. —Marsha Lawson, Pflugerville, Texas

      1 cup baking cocoa
      1 cup boiling water
      1 cup butter *or* margarine, softened
2-1/2 cups sugar
      4 eggs
      2 teaspoons vanilla extract
      3 cups cake flour
      2 teaspoons baking soda
  1/2 teaspoon baking powder
  1/2 teaspoon salt
      1 cup (8 ounces) sour cream
FROSTING:
      2 cups (12 ounces) semisweet chocolate chips
  1/2 cup butter *or* margarine
      1 cup (8 ounces) sour cream
      1 teaspoon vanilla extract
4-1/2 to 5 cups confectioners' sugar

Dissolve cocoa in water; set aside. In a mixing bowl, cream butter and sugar. Add eggs, one at a time, beating well after each. Add vanilla. Combine flour, baking soda, baking powder and salt; add to creamed mixture alternately with cocoa mixture and sour cream. Pour into three greased and floured 9-in. round baking pans. Bake at 350° for 30-35 minutes or until a toothpick inserted near the center comes out clean. Cool for 10 minutes; remove from pans to wire racks to cool completely.

In a heavy saucepan, melt chocolate chips and butter over low heat. Remove from the heat; cool for 5 minutes. Place in a mixing bowl; add sour cream and vanilla. Mix well. Add sugar; beat until light and fluffy. Spread between layers and over top and sides of cake. Refrigerate leftovers.
Yield: 16 servings.

Chocolate Angel Cake

(Pictured below)

When I married in 1944, I could barely boil water. My dear mother-in-law taught me her specialty—making the lightest of angel food cakes ever. This chocolate version is an easy, impressive treat. For many years, it was our son's choice for his birthday cake. —Joyce Shiffler
Manitou Springs, Colorado

1-1/2 cups confectioners' sugar
    1 cup cake flour
    1/4 cup baking cocoa
1-1/2 cups egg whites (about 10 eggs)
1-1/2 teaspoons cream of tartar
    1/2 teaspoon salt
    1 cup sugar
FROSTING:
1-1/2 cups whipping cream
    1/2 cup sugar
    1/4 cup baking cocoa
    1/2 teaspoon salt
    1/2 teaspoon vanilla extract

Sift together the confectioners' sugar, flour and cocoa three times; set aside. In a mixing bowl, beat egg whites, cream of tartar and salt until soft peaks form. Add sugar, 2 tablespoons at a time, beating until stiff peaks form. Gradually fold in the cocoa mixture, about a fourth at a time.

Spoon into an ungreased 10-in. tube pan. Carefully run a metal spatula or knife through batter to remove air pockets. Bake on lowest oven rack at 375° for 35-40 minutes or until the top springs back when lightly touched and cracks feel dry. Immediately invert pan; cool completely. Run a knife around edges and center tube to loosen; remove cake. In a mixing bowl, combine the first five frosting ingredients; cover and chill for 1 hour. Beat until stiff peaks form. Spread over top and sides of cake. Store in the refrigerator. **Yield:** 12-16 servings.

Chocolate Lover's Chiffon Cake

(Pictured above and on front cover)

Whenever there's a special occasion at our house, this cake is always requested—it is guaranteed to satisfy a craving for chocolate! —JoAnn Plate, Oskaloosa, Iowa

    1 cup egg whites (about 7 eggs)
    1/2 cup baking cocoa
    3/4 cup boiling water
1-3/4 cups cake flour
1-3/4 cups sugar
1-1/2 teaspoons baking soda
    1 teaspoon salt
    1/2 cup vegetable oil
    7 egg yolks
    2 teaspoons vanilla extract
    1/2 teaspoon cream of tartar
FILLING:
    3 cups whipping cream
1-1/2 cups confectioners' sugar
    3/4 cup baking cocoa
    2 teaspoons vanilla extract
    1/4 teaspoon salt

Place egg whites in a large mixing bowl; set aside for 30 minutes. Meanwhile, stir cocoa and water in a small bowl until smooth. Cool. In a large bowl, sift together flour, sugar, baking soda and salt. Make a well in the center; add oil, egg yolks, vanilla and cocoa mixture. Beat with a wooden spoon until smooth; set aside. Sprinkle cream of tartar over egg whites; beat until stiff peaks form. Fold into batter with a wire whisk. Pour into an ungreased 10-in. tube pan. Bake at 325° for 60-65 minutes or until top springs back when lightly touched. Immediately invert pan; cool completely. Run a knife around edges and center tube to loosen; remove cake.

For filling, combine all ingredients in a mixing bowl; refrigerate for 1 hour. Beat until stiff peaks form; refrigerate again. To fill cake, cut a 1-in. slice from top of cake; set aside. Using a sharp knife, carve a tunnel out of cake, leaving a 1-in.-thick wall on all sides; carefully remove cake. Fill tunnel with some of the filling; replace cake top. Frost top and sides of cake with remaining filling. Store in the refrigerator. **Yield:** 12 servings.

Cupid's Chocolate Cake

(Pictured below)

I'm pleased to share the recipe for the very best chocolate cake I have ever tasted. I prepare this treat every year on Valentine's Day. It's rich, delectable and absolutely irresistible. —Shelaine Duncan, North Powder, Oregon

    1 cup butter *or* margarine, softened
2-1/2 cups sugar
    4 eggs
2-1/2 teaspoons vanilla extract, *divided*
2-3/4 cups all-purpose flour
    1 cup baking cocoa
    2 teaspoons baking soda
1/2 teaspoon baking powder
1/2 teaspoon salt
    2 cups water
    1 cup whipping cream
1/4 cup confectioners' sugar
    4 cups buttercream frosting of your choice

In a mixing bowl, cream butter and sugar. Add the eggs, one at a time, beating well after each addition. Beat on high speed until light and fluffy. Stir in 1-1/2 teaspoons vanilla. Combine dry ingredients; add to the creamed mixture alternately with water. Pour into three greased and floured 9-in. round baking pans. Bake at 350° for 25-30 minutes or until a toothpick inserted near the center comes out clean. Cool for 10 minutes before removing from pans to wire racks to cool completely.

For filling, in a mixing bowl, beat cream until stiff peaks form. Beat in confectioners' sugar and remaining vanilla. Place bottom cake layer on a serving plate; spread with half of the filling. Repeat. Place top layer on cake; frost top and sides of cake with buttercream frosting. Store in the refrigerator. **Yield:** 12-14 servings.

Chocolate Chip Caramel Cake

(Pictured above)

When I want to serve a dessert that's pretty and delicious, I make this scrumptious cake. Dotted with chocolate chips and topped with caramel icing, pecans and a chocolate drizzle, it's a winning combination! —Michele VanDewerker, Roseboom, New York

    1 package (18-1/4 ounces) white cake mix
1-1/2 cups vanilla yogurt
    4 egg whites
    1 teaspoon baking soda
1/2 teaspoon baking powder
    1 cup miniature semisweet chocolate chips
CARAMEL TOPPING:
1/4 cup butter *or* margarine
1/3 cup packed brown sugar
    2 to 3 tablespoons evaporated milk
1/2 teaspoon vanilla extract
    1 cup confectioners' sugar
1/4 cup chopped pecans
CHOCOLATE DRIZZLE:
1/4 cup semisweet chocolate chips
1/2 teaspoon shortening

In a large mixing bowl, combine the first five ingredients. Beat on medium speed for 2 minutes. Stir in chocolate chips. Spread into a well-greased and floured 10-in. fluted tube pan. Bake at 350° for 50-55 minutes or until a toothpick inserted near the center comes out clean. Cool for 10 minutes; invert onto a wire rack to cool completely.

For topping, combine the butter and brown sugar in a saucepan; bring to a boil, stirring constantly. Boil for 2 minutes. Stir in milk and vanilla. Return to a boil; remove from the heat and cool slightly. Add sugar; beat on high with a portable mixer for 30 seconds or until thickened. Drizzle over cake. Sprinkle with nuts.

In a microwave oven, melt chocolate and shortening; stir until smooth. Drizzle over top. **Yield:** 12-16 servings.

Upside-Down German Chocolate Cake

(Pictured above)

This simple recipe yields a delectable German chocolate cake that folks will "flip over"! The tempting coconut and pecan "frosting" bakes under the batter and ends up on top when you turn the cake out of the pan.
—Mrs. Harold Sanders, Glouster, Ohio

1/2 cup packed brown sugar
1/4 cup butter *or* margarine
2/3 cup pecan halves
2/3 cup flaked coconut
1/4 cup evaporated milk
CAKE:
1/3 cup butter *or* margarine, softened
1 cup sugar
1 package (4 ounces) German sweet chocolate, melted
2 eggs
1 teaspoon vanilla extract
1-1/2 cups all-purpose flour
1/2 teaspoon baking soda
1/2 teaspoon baking powder
1/2 teaspoon salt
3/4 cup buttermilk
Whipped topping, optional

In a saucepan over low heat, cook and stir brown sugar and butter until sugar is dissolved and butter is melted. Spread into a greased 9-in. square baking pan. Sprinkle with pecans and coconut. Drizzle with milk; set aside.

In a mixing bowl, cream butter and sugar. Beat in the chocolate, eggs and vanilla. Combine the dry ingredients; add to the creamed mixture alternately with buttermilk. Pour over topping in pan. Bake at 350° for 40-45 minutes or until a toothpick inserted near the center comes out clean. Cool for 5 minutes before inverting onto a serving plate. Serve with whipped topping if desired. **Yield:** 9 servings.

Chocolate Cake with Fudge Sauce

(Pictured below)

My whole family makes sure to leave room for dessert when this wonderful cake is on the menu. We all love chocolate and agree this rich, quick and easy recipe is one of the yummiest ways to enjoy it.
—Lydia Briscoe
Scott Depot, West Virginia

1 package (3.4 ounces) cook-and-serve chocolate pudding/pie filling mix
2 cups milk
1 package (18-1/4 ounces) chocolate cake mix
SAUCE:
1/2 cup butter *or* margarine
1 cup (6 ounces) semisweet chocolate chips
1 can (12 ounces) evaporated milk
2 cups confectioners' sugar
1 teaspoon vanilla extract
Variegated mint, optional

In a saucepan or microwave oven, prepare pudding with milk according to package directions for pudding. Pour into a mixing bowl; add dry cake mix and beat until well blended. Spread into a greased 13-in. x 9-in. x 2-in. baking pan. Bake at 350° for 30-35 minutes or until cake springs back when lightly touched and edges pull away from sides of pan. Cool on a wire rack.

For sauce, in a heavy saucepan, melt butter and chocolate over low heat. Stir in evaporated milk and sugar until smooth. Bring to a boil over medium heat; cook and stir for 8 minutes or until thickened. Remove from the heat; stir in vanilla. Serve warm sauce over cake. If desired, garnish with mint. **Yield:** 12-15 servings.

White Chocolate Lime Mousse Cake

(Pictured below)

The line at the dessert table convinced me this cake was a winner when I served it at a party. It makes a pretty presentation, baking up nice and high. The zippy lime and gingersnap flavors really come through.
—Margery Richmond, Fort Collins, Colorado

   2 cups crushed gingersnaps (about 38 cookies)
   2 tablespoons sugar
1/3 cup butter *or* margarine, melted
FILLING:
   1 envelope unflavored gelatin
   6 tablespoons lime juice
   9 squares (1 ounce *each*) white baking chocolate, chopped
2-1/2 cups whipping cream, *divided*
   3 packages (8 ounces *each*) cream cheese, softened
   1 cup sugar
   1 tablespoon grated lime peel

Combine the gingersnaps, sugar and butter; press onto the bottom and 1 in. up the sides of a greased 9-in. springform pan. Set aside.

In a microwave-safe dish, sprinkle gelatin over lime juice. Let stand for 1 minute. Microwave on high for 10-20 seconds; stir until gelatin is dissolved. Set aside. In a heavy saucepan or microwave oven, melt chocolate with 1/2 cup cream; stir until smooth. Cool slightly; stir in dissolved gelatin.

In a mixing bowl, beat cream cheese and sugar until smooth. Gradually add chocolate mixture and lime peel; mix well. In another mixing bowl, beat the remaining cream until stiff peaks form. Gently fold into cream cheese mixture. Spoon over the crust. Cover and chill overnight. Refrigerate leftovers. **Yield:** 12-16 servings.

Tiny Cherry Cheesecakes

(Pictured above)

I prepare these mini cheesecakes every Christmas and for many weddings. I've received countless compliments and recipe requests. When I send these along in my husband's lunch, I have to be sure to pack extras because the men he works with love them, too.
—Janice Hertlein
Esterhazy, Saskatchewan

   1 cup all-purpose flour
1/3 cup sugar
1/4 cup baking cocoa
1/2 cup cold butter *or* margarine
   2 tablespoons cold water
FILLING:
   2 packages (3 ounces *each*) cream cheese, softened
1/4 cup sugar
   2 tablespoons milk
   1 teaspoon vanilla extract
   1 egg
   1 can (21 ounces) cherry *or* strawberry pie filling

In a small bowl, combine flour, sugar and cocoa; cut in butter until crumbly. Gradually add water, tossing with a fork until dough forms a ball. Shape into 24 balls. Place in greased miniature muffin cups; press dough onto the bottom and up the sides of each cup.

In a mixing bowl, beat cream cheese and sugar until smooth. Beat in milk and vanilla. Add egg; beat on low just until combined. Spoon about 1 tablespoonful into each cup. Bake at 325° for 15-18 minutes or until set. Cool on a wire rack for 30 minutes. Carefully remove from pans to cool completely. Top with pie filling. Store in the refrigerator. **Yield:** 2 dozen.

Turtle Cheesecake

(Pictured below)

Our guests love this rich, delicious make-ahead dessert. It turns out every time and is impressive on the table.
—Jo Groth, Plainfield, Iowa

- 2 cups vanilla wafer crumbs
- 1/2 cup butter *or* margarine, melted
- 1 package (14 ounces) caramels
- 1 can (5 ounces) evaporated milk
- 2 cups chopped pecans, toasted, *divided*
- 4 packages (8 ounces *each*) cream cheese, softened
- 1 cup sugar
- 2 teaspoons vanilla extract
- 4 eggs
- 1 cup (6 ounces) semisweet chocolate chips, melted and slightly cooled

Whipped cream, optional

In a small bowl, combine crumbs and butter; mix well. Press onto the bottom and 2 in. up the sides of a 10-in. springform pan. Place on a baking sheet. Bake at 350° for 8-10 minutes; cool on a wire rack.

In a saucepan over low heat, melt caramels in milk, stirring until smooth. Cool 5 minutes. Pour into crust; top with 1-1/2 cups of pecans. In a mixing bowl, beat cream cheese until smooth. Add sugar and vanilla; mix well. Add eggs; beat on low speed just until combined. Add chocolate; mix just until blended. Carefully spread over pecans. Bake at 350° for 55-65 minutes or until center is almost set. Cool on a wire rack for 10 minutes. Carefully run a knife around the edge of pan to loosen; cool 1 hour longer. Refrigerate overnight. Remove sides of pan. Garnish with whipped cream and remaining pecans if desired. Refrigerate leftovers. **Yield:** 16 servings.

Peanut Butter Chocolate Cake

(Pictured above)

Since chocolate and peanut butter are two of my grand-daughters' favorite flavors, I frequently fix this cake as a finale to my meals. —Elaine Medeiros, Wamego, Kansas

- 2-1/4 cups all-purpose flour
- 1-1/2 cups sugar
- 1/3 cup baking cocoa
- 1-1/2 teaspoons baking soda
- 1/2 teaspoon salt
- 1-1/2 cups water
- 1/2 cup vegetable oil
- 4-1/2 teaspoons white vinegar
- 1-1/2 teaspoons vanilla extract

PEANUT BUTTER BATTER:
- 4 ounces cream cheese, softened
- 1/4 cup creamy peanut butter
- 1/3 cup plus 1 tablespoon sugar, *divided*
- 1 egg
- 1/8 teaspoon salt
- 1/2 cup semisweet chocolate chips
- 1/2 cup chopped pecans

In a large bowl, combine the flour, sugar, cocoa, baking soda and salt. Stir in water, oil, vinegar and vanilla; mix well. Pour into a greased 13-in. x 9-in. x 2-in. baking pan.

In a mixing bowl, beat cream cheese, peanut butter, 1/3 cup sugar, egg and salt until smooth. Stir in chocolate chips. Drop by tablespoonfuls over cake batter; cut through batter with a knife to swirl the peanut butter mixture. Sprinkle with pecans and remaining sugar.

Bake at 350° for 30-35 minutes or until a toothpick inserted near the center comes out clean. Cool on a wire rack before cutting. Refrigerate leftovers. **Yield:** 24 servings.

Texas Cake

(Pictured on front cover)

This "Texas-sized" sheet cake is great for large groups and parties—it's an often-requested birthday cake around our dairy farm. —Lynn Rogers, Lyon, Michigan

- 2 cups all-purpose flour
- 2 cups sugar
- 1/2 teaspoon salt

    1 teaspoon baking soda
    1 teaspoon ground cinnamon
    1 cup butter *or* margarine
    1 cup water
    3 tablespoons baking cocoa
    2 eggs
  1/2 cup sour milk*
    1 teaspoon vanilla extract
FROSTING:
    5 tablespoons all-purpose flour
    1 cup milk
  1/2 cup shortening
  1/2 cup butter *or* margarine
    1 cup sugar
    1 teaspoon vanilla extract
  1/2 teaspoon salt

Combine the first five ingredients in a large mixing bowl; set aside. In a heavy saucepan, bring butter, water and cocoa to a boil; add to dry ingredients and mix well. Mix in eggs, milk and vanilla. Pour into a greased 15-in. x 10-in. x 1-in. baking pan. Bake at 350° for 25-30 minutes or until a toothpick inserted near the center comes out clean.

For frosting, dissolve flour in milk; cook in a heavy saucepan until thick, stirring occasionally. Cool. In a small mixing bowl, cream remaining ingredients for 4 minutes. Add flour/milk mixture and beat until fluffy, about 2-3 minutes. Frost cake. **Yield:** 15-20 servings.

*Editor's Note: To sour milk, add 1-1/2 teaspoons vinegar to 1/2 cup milk.

Chocolate Strawberry Torte

(Pictured on page 48)

I made this beauty one year for my father-in-law's birthday and it was a hit. I've made it since for Easter and other spring occasions. —Paula Magnus, Republic, Washington

    5 squares (1 ounce *each*) semisweet chocolate
  3/4 cup butter (no substitutes)
1-1/2 cups sugar
    3 eggs
    2 teaspoons vanilla extract
2-1/2 cups all-purpose flour
    1 teaspoon baking soda
  1/4 teaspoon salt
1-1/2 cups water
STRAWBERRY FILLING:
    4 cups sliced fresh strawberries
    2 tablespoons sugar
    1 teaspoon vanilla extract
GLAZE:
    3 squares (1 ounce *each*) semisweet chocolate
    1 tablespoon butter
    1 cup confectioners' sugar
    3 tablespoons water
  1/2 teaspoon vanilla extract
    1 carton (8 ounces) frozen whipped topping, thawed

In a microwave oven or heavy saucepan, melt chocolate and butter; stir until smooth. Transfer to a large mixing bowl; add sugar. Add the eggs, one at a time, beating well after each addition. Beat in vanilla. Combine the flour, baking soda and salt; add to chocolate mixture alternately with water and beat until smooth.

Pour into two greased and floured 9-in. round baking pans. Bake at 350° for 28-33 minutes or until a toothpick inserted near the center comes out clean. Cool for 10 minutes before removing from pans to wire racks.

In a bowl, combine filling ingredients; set aside. For glaze, in a microwave oven or heavy saucepan, melt chocolate and butter. Stir in confectioners' sugar, water and vanilla until smooth. Cool slightly.

To assemble, place one cake layer on a serving plate. Spread with half of the whipped topping; drizzle with half of the glaze. Top with half of the filling. Repeat layers. **Yield:** 10-12 servings.

Classic Chocolate Cake

(Pictured below)

This recipe appeared on a can of Hershey's Cocoa way back in 1943. I tried it, my boys liked it and I've been making it ever since. —Betty Follas, Morgan Hill, California

  2/3 cup butter *or* margarine, softened
1-2/3 cups sugar
    3 eggs
    2 cups all-purpose flour
  2/3 cup baking cocoa
1-1/4 teaspoons baking soda
    1 teaspoon salt
1-1/3 cups milk
Frosting of your choice

In a mixing bowl, cream butter and sugar until fluffy. Add eggs, one at a time, beating well after each addition. Combine flour, cocoa, baking soda and salt; add to creamed mixture alternately with milk, beating until smooth after each addition. Pour batter into a greased and floured 13-in. x 9-in. x 2-in. baking pan. Bake at 350° for 35-40 minutes or until a toothpick inserted near the center comes out clean. Cool on a wire rack. Frost with the frosting of your choice. **Yield:** 12-15 servings.

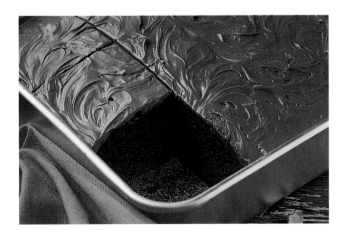

Macadamia Fudge Cake

(Pictured above)

Our daughter and her husband operate a cookie factory in Hawaii. After she sent a big supply of macadamia nuts, I came up with this cake I make for church dinners and ladies lunches. —Marguerite Gough, Salida, Colorado

1/2 cup butter *or* margarine, softened
3/4 cup sugar
1 egg
3/4 cup sour cream
1/2 teaspoon vanilla extract
1 cup all-purpose flour
1/4 cup baking cocoa
1-1/2 teaspoons instant coffee granules
1/2 teaspoon baking powder
1/2 teaspoon baking soda
1/4 teaspoon salt
TOPPING:
1 cup (6 ounces) semisweet chocolate chips
2/3 cup whipping cream
1/2 cup sugar
2 tablespoons butter *or* margarine
2 tablespoons corn syrup
1 teaspoon vanilla extract
1-1/2 cups coarsely chopped macadamia
nuts *or* almonds

In a mixing bowl, cream butter and sugar until fluffy. Beat in egg, sour cream and vanilla. Combine flour, cocoa, coffee, baking powder, baking soda and salt; add to creamed mixture and mix well. Pour into a greased 9-in. round baking pan. Bake at 350° for 30 minutes or until a toothpick inserted near the center comes out clean. Cool for 10 minutes; remove from pan to a wire rack to cool completely.

For topping, combine chocolate chips, cream, sugar, butter and corn syrup in a saucepan; bring to a boil, stirring constantly. Reduce heat to medium; cook and stir for 7 minutes. Remove from the heat; stir in vanilla. Cool for 10-15 minutes. Beat with a wooden spoon until slightly thickened, about 4-5 minutes. Stir in nuts. Place cake on a serving plate; pour topping over cake. **Yield:** 8-10 servings.

Incredible Chocolate Cake

This incredible-tasting chocolate cake is wonderfully easy to make! Everyone thinks I spent hours in the kitchen on it. —Janice Britz, Lexington, Michigan

1 package (18-1/4 ounces) chocolate cake mix
1 can (14 ounces) sweetened condensed milk
1 jar (12-1/4 ounces) caramel ice cream topping
1 carton (12 ounces) frozen whipped topping, thawed
2 tablespoons baking cocoa
2 Heath candy bars (1.4 ounces *each*), crushed

Prepare and bake cake mix according to package directions, using a greased 13-in. x 9-in. x 2-in. baking pan. Place on a wire rack for 10 minutes. Using the end of a wooden spoon handle, poke 20 holes in warm cake. Pour milk over cake; cool for 10 minutes. Pour caramel topping over cake; cool completely.

In a bowl, combine whipped topping and cocoa; spread over cake. Sprinkle with crushed candy bars. Cover and store in the refrigerator. **Yield:** 12-15 servings.

Mint Chocolate Cake

(Pictured below)

My husband works for a mint farmer, so I'm always looking for recipes with mint in them. I received this recipe at my bridal shower. My friend wrote "Easy and pretty" on the top corner of the recipe card—and it's so true. —Virginia Horst, Mesa, Washington

1 package (18-1/4 ounces) chocolate cake mix
FROSTING:
1/2 cup butter *or* margarine, softened
2 cups confectioners' sugar
1 tablespoon water
1/2 teaspoon peppermint extract
3 drops green food coloring

TOPPING:

1-1/2 cups milk chocolate chips
6 tablespoons butter *or* margarine, softened
1/4 teaspoon peppermint extract

Prepare cake batter according to package directions. Pour into a greased 15-in. x 10-in. x 1-in. baking pan. Bake at 350° for 25-30 minutes or until a toothpick inserted near the center comes out clean. Cool on a wire rack.

In a bowl, combine the frosting ingredients until smooth. Spread over cooled cake. For topping, in a microwave-safe bowl, melt chocolate chips and butter; stir in extract. Spread over frosting. Refrigerate until set. **Yield:** 20-24 servings.

Double Chocolate Torte

(Pictured below)

If you love chocolate, you won't be able to resist this rich, fudgy torte. I often make it for company because it's easy to prepare yet looks so impressive. For special occasions, I place it on a fancy cake plate and I use a can of whipped topping to decorate it. It looks and tastes awesome!
—Naomi Treadwell, Swans Island, Maine

1 package fudge brownie mix (13-inch x 9-inch pan size)
1 cup (6 ounces) semisweet chocolate chips, melted
1/2 cup butter *or* margarine, softened
2 cups whipped topping
1 teaspoon chocolate sprinkles

Prepare brownie mix according to package directions for fudge-like brownies. Spread batter in a greased and floured 9-in. round baking pan. Bake at 350° for 38-42 minutes or until center springs back when lightly touched.

Cool for 10 minutes. Invert onto a serving plate; cool completely. In a bowl, stir the chocolate and butter until smooth. Spread over brownie layer; refrigerate for 30 minutes. Just before serving, top with whipped topping. Decorate with sprinkles. **Yield:** 9-12 servings.

Chocolate Chip Cookie Dough Cheesecake

(Pictured above)

I created this recipe to combine two of my all-time favorites—cheesecake for the grown-up in me and chocolate chip cookie dough for the little girl in me. Sour cream offsets the sweetness and adds a nice tang. Everyone who tries this scrumptious treat loves it.
—Julie Craig
Jackson, Wisconsin

1-3/4 cups crushed chocolate chip cookies
or chocolate wafer crumbs
1/4 cup sugar
1/3 cup butter *or* margarine, melted
FILLING:
3 packages (8 ounces *each*) cream cheese, softened
1 cup sugar
3 eggs
1 cup (8 ounces) sour cream
1/2 teaspoon vanilla extract
COOKIE DOUGH:
1/4 cup butter *or* margarine, softened
1/4 cup sugar
1/4 cup packed brown sugar
1 tablespoon water
1 teaspoon vanilla extract
1/2 cup all-purpose flour
1-1/2 cups miniature semisweet chocolate chips, *divided*

In a small bowl, combine cookie crumbs and sugar; stir in butter. Press onto the bottom and 1 in. up the sides of a greased 9-in. springform pan; set aside.

In a mixing bowl, beat cream cheese and sugar until smooth. Add eggs; beat on low just until combined. Add sour cream and vanilla; beat just until blended. Pour over crust; set aside. In another mixing bowl, cream butter and sugars on medium speed for 3 minutes. Add water and vanilla. Gradually add flour. Stir in 1 cup chocolate chips. Drop dough by teaspoonfuls over filling, gently pushing dough below surface (dough should be completely covered by filling). Place pan on a baking sheet.

Bake at 350° for 45-55 minutes or until center is almost set. Cool on a wire rack for 10 minutes. Carefully run a knife around edge of pan to loosen; cool 1 hour longer. Refrigerate overnight; remove sides of pan. Sprinkle with remaining chips. **Yield:** 12-14 servings.

Heart's Delight Torte

(Pictured at right)

Cherry pie filling dresses up homemade chocolate cake layers in this impressive dessert. Our family enjoys it so much.
—Nancy Heesch, Sioux Falls, South Dakota

1/3 cup shortening
1 cup sugar
1 egg
3/4 cup buttermilk
1 teaspoon vanilla extract
1 cup plus 2 tablespoons all-purpose flour
1/3 cup baking cocoa
1/2 teaspoon baking soda
1/2 teaspoon salt
2 cans (21 ounces *each*) cherry pie filling
1 cup whipped topping
2 tablespoons semisweet chocolate chips

In a mixing bowl, cream shortening and sugar. Add the egg, buttermilk and vanilla. Combine the dry ingredients; gradually add to creamed mixture. Pour into a greased 9-in. heart-shaped or round baking pan. Bake at 350° for 30-35 minutes or until a toothpick inserted near the center comes out clean. Cool for 10 minutes before removing from pan to a wire rack to cool completely.

Split cake in half; place one layer on a serving plate. Spread with one can of pie filling; top with second cake layer. Pipe whipped topping around edge; garnish with chocolate chips. Spoon cherries from the second can of pie filling onto the top of the cake (refrigerate any remaining filling for another use). **Yield:** 10-12 servings.

Chocolate Almond Cheesecake

(Pictured below)

Everyone saves room for dessert when this cheesecake is part of the menu. Its rich chocolate flavor is so satisfying when we're craving something sweet and creamy.
—Jeri Dobrowski, Beach, North Dakota

1-1/4 cups graham cracker crumbs
1-1/2 cups sugar, *divided*
1/2 cup plus 2 tablespoons baking cocoa, *divided*
1/4 cup butter *or* margarine, melted
2 packages (8 ounces *each*) cream cheese, softened
1 cup (8 ounces) sour cream
3 eggs
1-1/2 teaspoons almond extract, *divided*
1 cup whipping cream
1/4 cup confectioners' sugar
1/4 cup sliced almonds, toasted

Combine crumbs, 1/4 cup sugar, 2 tablespoons cocoa and butter; mix well. Press onto the bottom of a 9-in. springform pan; chill.

In a mixing bowl, beat the cream cheese, sour cream and remaining sugar until smooth. Add eggs; beat on low just until combined. Stir in 1 teaspoon of extract and remaining cocoa. Pour into crust. Place on a baking sheet. Bake at 350° for 45-50 minutes or until the center is almost set. Cool on a wire rack for 10 minutes. Carefully run a knife around the edge of pan to loosen; cool 1 hour longer. Refreigerate overnight. Remove sides of pan.

In a mixing bowl, whip cream until it mounds slightly. Add confectioners' sugar and remaining extract; continue whipping until soft peaks form. Spread evenly over cheesecake. Sprinkle with almonds. Store in refrigerator. **Yield:** 12 servings.

No-Bake Chocolate Cheesecake

Cooking and collecting new recipes are my favorite hobbies. Since I discovered this one around 5 years ago, my family's requested it often. It's so creamy and rich you won't believe it has only five ingredients. *—Michelle Overton*
Oak Ridge, Tennessee

1-1/2 cups semisweet chocolate chips
2 packages (one 8 ounces, one 3 ounces) cream cheese, softened
1/4 cup sugar
1 carton (8 ounces) frozen whipped topping, thawed
1 chocolate crumb crust (9 inches)

Melt the chocolate chips in a microwave oven or double boiler; stir until smooth. In a mixing bowl, beat cream cheese and sugar. Beat in melted chocolate and whipped topping at low speed. Pour into the crust. Cover and refrigerate for at least 4 hours. **Yield:** 6-8 servings.

Chocolate Chocolate Chip Cake

(Pictured above)

This is a chocolate lover's dream! It will definitely satisfy any chocolate craving you may have. I often make this cake for birthdays or other special occasions.
—Roni Goodell, Spanish Fork, Utah

    1 cup shortening
    2 cups sugar
    4 squares (1 ounce *each*) unsweetened chocolate, melted and cooled
    2 teaspoons vanilla extract
    5 eggs
2-1/4 cups cake flour
    1 teaspoon baking soda
    1 teaspoon salt
    1 cup buttermilk
    2 cups (12 ounces) semisweet chocolate chips
FROSTING:
  2/3 cup butter *or* margarine, softened
5-1/3 cups confectioners' sugar
    1 cup baking cocoa
    1 cup milk
    2 teaspoons vanilla extract

In a mixing bowl, cream shortening and sugar. Add chocolate and vanilla; mix well. Add eggs, one at a time, beating well after each addition. Combine flour, baking soda and salt; add to creamed mixture alternately with buttermilk. Fold in the chocolate chips. Pour into three greased and floured 9-in. round baking pans. Bake at 350° for 30-35 minutes or until a toothpick inserted near the center comes out clean. Cool for 10 minutes; remove from pans to wire racks to cool completely.

In a mixing bowl, cream butter. Combine sugar and cocoa; add to creamed mixture alternately with milk. Add vanilla; beat well. Frost between layers and top and sides of cake. **Yield:** 12 servings.

Fudgy Raspberry Torte

(Pictured below)

Guests will think you fussed when you serve this three-layer torte made with convenient cake and pudding mixes, a bit of jam and fresh raspberries. It looks elegant for most any special occasion and always brings lots of compliments.   *—Dolores Hurtt, Florence, Montana*

    1 package (18-1/4 ounces) chocolate fudge cake mix
1-1/3 cups water
    3 eggs
  1/3 cup vegetable oil
  3/4 cup ground pecans
1-1/2 cups cold milk
    1 package (3.9 ounces) instant chocolate fudge *or* chocolate pudding mix
  1/2 cup seedless raspberry jam
1-1/2 cups whipped topping
  1/4 cup finely chopped pecans
Fresh raspberries

In a mixing bowl, combine dry cake mix, water, eggs and oil; mix well. Add ground pecans; mix just until combined. Pour into three greased and floured 9-in. round baking pans. Bake at 350° for 15-20 minutes or until a toothpick inserted near the center comes out clean. Cool for 10 minutes before removing from pans to wire racks to cool completely.

In a mixing bowl, beat milk and pudding mix on low speed for 2 minutes or until thickened. In a saucepan, melt jam. Brush over the top of each cake. Place one cake on a serving plate; spread with half of the pudding. Repeat layers. Top with third cake layer; spread top with whipped topping. Sprinkle with chopped pecans. Garnish with raspberries. Store in the refrigerator. **Yield:** 12 servings.

Chocolate Praline Torte

(Pictured above)

No one will know this fancy dessert started with a handy boxed cake mix. We enjoy the scrumptious treat throughout the year for special dinners, potlucks and even picnics.
—Sandra Castillo, Watertown, Wisconsin

- 1 cup packed brown sugar
- 1/2 cup butter (no substitutes)
- 1/4 cup whipping cream
- 3/4 cup coarsely chopped pecans
- 1 package (18-1/4 ounces) devil's food cake mix
TOPPING:
- 1-3/4 cups whipping cream
- 1/4 cup confectioners' sugar
- 1/4 teaspoon vanilla extract
Chocolate curls, optional

In a saucepan, combine brown sugar, butter and cream. Stir over low heat until butter is melted. Pour into two greased 9-in. round baking pans. Sprinkle with pecans; set aside. Prepare cake mix according to package directions. Carefully pour batter over pecans. Bake at 325° for 35-45 minutes or until a toothpick inserted near the center comes out clean. Cool in pans for 10 minutes; invert onto wire racks to cool completely.

For topping, beat cream in a mixing bowl until soft peaks form. Add sugar and vanilla; beat until stiff. Place one cake layer, pecan side up, on a serving plate. Spread with half of the topping. Top with second cake layer and remaining topping. Garnish with chocolate curls if desired. Store in the refrigerator. **Yield:** 8-10 servings.

Chocolate Cheesecake

(Pictured on page 48)

Everyone's a chocolate lover when it comes to this special dessert. "It melts in your mouth!" and "Very smooth and fudgy!" are typical comments I've heard after guests take a bite. For a fun taste twist, spoon cherry or strawberry

topping over each individual slice of cheesecake. It's delicious and pretty.   *—Sue Call, Beech Grove, Indiana*

- 1 cup crushed chocolate wafer crumbs
- 3 tablespoons sugar
- 3 tablespoons butter *or* margarine, melted
FILLING:
- 2 cups (12 ounces) semisweet chocolate chips
- 2 packages (8 ounces *each*) cream cheese, softened
- 3/4 cup sugar
- 2 tablespoons all-purpose flour
- 2 eggs
- 1 teaspoon vanilla extract
Strawberries and white chocolate shavings, optional

In a small bowl, combine cookie crumbs and sugar; stir in butter. Press onto the bottom of a greased 9-in. springform pan; set aside. In a saucepan over low heat, melt the chocolate chips; stir until smooth. Set aside.

In a mixing bowl, beat cream cheese and sugar until smooth. Add flour; beat well. Add eggs; beat on low just until combined. Stir in vanilla and melted chocolate just until blended. Pour over crust. Place pan on a baking sheet.

Bake at 350° for 40-45 minutes or until center is almost set. Cool on a wire rack for 10 minutes. Carefully run a knife around edge of pan to loosen; cool 1 hour longer. Refrigerate overnight. Remove sides of pan. Garnish slices with strawberries and chocolate shavings if desired. Refrigerate leftovers. **Yield:** 12 servings.

Decadent Fudge Cake

(Pictured below and on front cover)

Everyone I serve it to seems to love the rich flavor of this attractive cake. Four types of chocolate make it decadent.
—Anna Hogge, Yorktown, Virginia

- 1 cup butter *or* margarine, softened
- 1-1/2 cups sugar
- 4 eggs
- 1 cup buttermilk
- 1/2 teaspoon baking soda

2-1/2 cups all-purpose flour
  2 bars (4 ounces *each*) German sweet chocolate, melted
  1 cup chocolate syrup
  2 teaspoons vanilla extract
1-1/4 cups semisweet chocolate mini-morsels, *divided*
  4 squares (1 ounce *each*) white baking chocolate, chopped
  2 tablespoons plus 1 teaspoon shortening, *divided*

Cream butter in a large mixing bowl. Gradually mix in sugar. Add eggs, one at a time, beating well after each addition. Combine buttermilk and baking soda; add to creamed mixture alternately with flour, beginning and ending with flour. Add melted chocolate, chocolate syrup and vanilla. Stir in 1 cup mini-morsels. Pour into a greased and floured 10-in. fluted tube pan. Bake at 325° for 1 hour and 15 minutes or until a toothpick comes out clean. Immediately invert cake onto a serving plate; cool completely.

Meanwhile, combine white chocolate and 2 tablespoons shortening in the top of a double boiler. Bring water to a boil; reduce heat to low and cook until mixture is melted and smooth. Remove from heat and cool slightly; drizzle over cake. Melt remaining mini-morsels and shortening in a small saucepan over low heat, stirring until smooth. Remove from heat; cool slightly Drizzle over white chocolate. **Yield:** 16-20 servings.

Brownie Swirl Cheesecake

(Pictured on page 48)

It may look fancy, but this cheesecake is so simple. The secret is the speedy crust—it's from a packaged brownie mix! You don't need to be an experienced cook to make the elegant chocolate swirls on top—anyone can do it.
—*Janet Brunner, Burlington, Kentucky*

  1 package (8 ounces) brownie mix*
  2 packages (8 ounces *each*) cream cheese, softened
1/2 cup sugar
  1 teaspoon vanilla extract
  2 eggs
  1 cup milk chocolate chips, melted
Whipped cream and miniature chocolate kisses, optional

Prepare brownie mix according to package directions for chewy fudge brownies. Spread into a greased 9-in. springform pan. Bake at 350° for 15 minutes (brownies will not test done). Cool for 10 minutes on a wire rack.

Meanwhile, in a mixing bowl, combine cream cheese, sugar and vanilla; mix well. Add eggs; beat on low speed just until combined. Pour over the brownie crust. Top with melted chocolate; cut through batter with a knife to swirl the chocolate. Place pan on a baking sheet. Bake at 350° for 35-40 minutes or until center is almost set. Cool on a wire rack for 10 minutes. Run a knife around edge of pan

to loosen; cool completely. Remove sides of pan; refrigerate for at least 3 hours. Garnish with whipped cream and chocolate kisses if desired. **Yield:** 8-10 servings.

*Editor's Note: This recipe was tested with Jiffy brand fudge brownie mix.

Orange Chocolate Cheesecake

(Pictured above)

White chocolate and oranges are perfect together in this dessert. —*Tangee Bradley, Columbia, South Carolina*

  2 cups vanilla wafer crumbs
  6 tablespoons butter *or* margarine, melted
1/4 cup sugar
FILLING:
  4 packages (8 ounces *each*) cream cheese, softened
  1 cup sugar
  4 eggs
  1 cup (8 ounces) sour cream
10 squares (1 ounce *each*) white baking chocolate, melted
TOPPING:
  1 cup (8 ounces) sour cream
  3 tablespoons sugar
1/2 to 1 teaspoon orange extract
  2 cans (11 ounces *each*) mandarin oranges, well drained

In a bowl, combine the first three ingredients; mix well. Press onto the bottom and 1-1/2 in. up the sides of a greased 10-in. springform pan. Place on a baking sheet. Bake at 350° for 10 minutes; cool completely.

In a mixing bowl, beat cream cheese, sugar, eggs and sour cream just until blended. Add chocolate. Pour into crust. Place on a baking sheet. Bake at 350° for 1 to 1-1/4 hours or until center is nearly set. Cool to room temperature, about 2 hours.

Combine sour cream, sugar and extract; spread over filling. Bake at 450° for 5-7 minutes or until set. Chill, uncovered, 1 hour. Arrange oranges on cheesecake. Cover and chill at least 4 hours. **Yield:** 12-16 servings.

Black Forest Torte

(Pictured below)

I like to serve this pretty dessert at holiday meals, especially Christmas. Guests are always impressed.
—Glatis McNiel, Constantine, Michigan

1-1/3 cups all-purpose flour
1-3/4 cups sugar
1-1/4 teaspoons baking soda
  1/4 teaspoon baking powder
  2/3 cup butter (no substitutes)
    4 squares (1 ounce *each*) unsweetened chocolate
1-1/4 cups water
    1 teaspoon vanilla extract
    3 eggs
CHOCOLATE FILLING:
    2 packages (4 ounces *each*) German sweet
      chocolate, *divided*
  3/4 cup butter
  1/2 cup chopped pecans
CREAM FILLING:
    2 cups whipping cream
    1 tablespoon confectioners' sugar
    1 teaspoon vanilla extract

In a mixing bowl, combine flour, sugar, baking soda and baking powder. In a saucepan, melt butter and chocolate; cool. Pour chocolate mixture, water and vanilla into flour mixture. Beat on low for 1 minute, then on medium for 2 minutes. Add eggs, one at a time, beating well after each. Divide batter among two 9-in. round baking pans that have been greased, floured and lined with waxed paper. Bake at 350° for 25-30 minutes or until a toothpick inserted near the center comes out clean. Cool in pans 10 minutes. Remove to a wire rack.

For chocolate filling, melt 1-1/2 packages of German chocolate over low heat. Stir in butter and nuts. Watching closely, cool filling just until it reaches spreading consistency. For cream filling, whip cream with sugar and vanilla until stiff peaks form.

To assemble, slice cooled cake layers in half horizontally. Place one bottom layer on a serving platter; cover with half of the chocolate filling. Top with a second cake layer; spread on half of the cream filling. Repeat layers. Grate remaining German chocolate; sprinkle on the top. Refrigerate until serving. **Yield:** 12-16 servings.

Neapolitan Cheesecake

(Pictured above)

This rich, creamy cheesecake is a crowd-pleasing standout. It has won first-place ribbons at numerous fairs and years later it's still my family's favorite dessert.
—Sherri Regalbuto, Carp, Ontario

    1 cup chocolate wafer crumbs
    5 tablespoons butter *or* margarine, melted, *divided*
    3 packages (8 ounces *each*) cream cheese, softened
  3/4 cup sugar
    3 eggs
    1 teaspoon vanilla extract
    5 squares (1 ounce *each*) semisweet
      chocolate, *divided*
2-1/2 squares (2-1/2 ounces) white baking
      chocolate, *divided*
  1/3 cup mashed sweetened strawberries
    2 teaspoons shortening, *divided*

Combine crumbs and 3 tablespoons of butter; press onto the bottom of an ungreased 9-in. springform pan. Place pan on a baking sheet. Bake at 350° for 8 minutes; cool on a wire rack.

In a mixing bowl, beat the cream cheese and sugar until smooth. Add eggs; beat on low speed just until combined. Add vanilla. Divide into three portions, about 1-2/3 cups each.

Melt 2 squares semisweet chocolate; stir into one portion of batter. Melt 2 squares of white chocolate; stir into second portion. Stir strawberries into remaining batter. Spread semisweet mixture evenly over crust. Carefully spread with white chocolate mixture, then strawberry mixture. Place on a baking sheet. Bake at 425° for 10 minutes; reduce heat to 300°. Bake 50-55 minutes or until center is nearly set. Remove from oven; immediately run a knife around edge. Cool; remove from pan.

Melt remaining semisweet chocolate, remaining butter and 1 teaspoon of shortening; cool for 2 minutes. Pour over cake. Melt remaining white chocolate and shortening; drizzle over glaze. Refrigerate leftovers. **Yield:** 12-14 servings.

Deluxe Chip Cheesecake

(Pictured on page 48)

My husband and I love cheesecake. Once, when we were asked to make a dessert for a "traveling basket" for our church, we prepared this luscious layered treat. It looked so good, we couldn't bear to give it away. We ended up contributing another sweet treat instead! —Kari Gollup
Madison, Wisconsin

1-1/2 cups vanilla wafer crumbs
  1/2 cup confectioners' sugar
  1/4 cup baking cocoa
  1/3 cup butter *or* margarine, melted
FILLING:
   3 packages (8 ounces *each*) cream cheese, softened
  3/4 cup sugar
  1/3 cup sour cream
   3 tablespoons all-purpose flour
   1 teaspoon vanilla extract
  1/4 teaspoon salt
   3 eggs
   1 cup (6 ounces) butterscotch chips, melted
   1 cup (6 ounces) semisweet chocolate chips, melted
   1 cup (6 ounces) vanilla *or* white chips, melted
TOPPING:
   1 tablespoon *each* butterscotch, semisweet and vanilla chips
1-1/2 teaspoons shortening

In a bowl, combine wafer crumbs, confectioners' sugar, cocoa and butter. Press onto the bottom and 1-1/2 in. up the sides of a greased 9-in. springform pan. Place pan on baking sheet. Bake at 350° for 7-9 minutes. Cool on a wire rack.

In a mixing bowl, beat cream cheese and sugar until smooth. Add sour cream, flour, vanilla and salt; mix well. Add eggs; beat on low speed just until combined. Remove 1-1/2 cups batter to a bowl; stir in butterscotch chips. Pour over crust. Add chocolate chips to another 1-1/2 cups batter; carefully spoon over butterscotch layer. Stir vanilla chips into remaining batter; spoon over chocolate layer.

Bake at 350° for 55-60 minutes or until center is almost set. Cool on a wire rack for 10 minutes. Carefully run a knife around edge of pan to loosen. Cool for 1 hour.

For topping, place each flavor of chips and 1/2 teaspoon shortening in three small microwave-safe bowls. Microwave on high for 25 seconds; stir. Heat in 10- to 20-second intervals, stirring until smooth. Drizzle over cheesecake. Chill for at least 3 hours. Remove sides of pan. Refrigerate leftovers. **Yield:** 12-14 servings.

Nutty Fudge Torte

(Pictured at right)

This dessert is so yummy and beautiful, you'd never guess it's easy to make (it starts with a convenient packaged cake mix). Rich, moist and fudgy, it never fails to draw compliments from family and friends...as well as requests for the recipe. I'm always happy to oblige! —Kay Berg
Lopez Island, Washington

  1/2 cup semisweet chocolate chips
  1/3 cup sweetened condensed milk
   1 package (18-1/4 ounces) devil's food cake mix
  1/3 cup vegetable oil
   1 teaspoon ground cinnamon
   1 can (15 ounces) sliced pears, drained
   2 eggs
  1/3 cup chopped pecans, toasted
   2 teaspoons water
  1/4 cup hot caramel ice cream topping, warmed
  1/2 teaspoon milk
Whipped cream *or* vanilla ice cream and additional toasted pecans, optional

In a microwave oven, melt chocolate chips with condensed milk; stir until smooth. Set aside. In a mixing bowl, combine cake mix, oil and cinnamon until crumbly. Set aside 1/2 cup for topping. In a blender or food processor, process pears until smooth; add to remaining cake mixture with eggs. Beat on medium speed for 2 minutes. Pour into a greased 9-in. springform pan. Drop melted chocolate by tablespoonfuls over batter.

Combine pecans, water and reserved cake mixture; crumble over chocolate. Bake at 350° for 45-50 minutes or until a toothpick inserted near the center comes out clean. Cool for 10 minutes. Carefully run a knife around sides of pan to loosen. Cool completely on a wire rack. Remove sides of pan.

Combine caramel topping and milk until smooth; drizzle on serving plates. Top with a slice of torte. If desired, serve with whipped cream or ice cream and sprinkle with pecans. **Yield:** 12-14 servings.

CHOCOLATE MINT DESSERT, PAGE 70

CHOCOLATE MALTED ICE CREAM, PAGE 68

SWEETHEART BROWNIE SUNDAE, PAGE 72

GERMAN CHOCOLATE ICE CREAM, PAGE 71

Ice Cream
Treats & Sauces

Chocolate Praline Ice Cream Topping

(Pictured above)

Friends tell me they look forward to ice cream socials just to have this topping. —Angie Zalewski
Dripping Springs, Texas

    1 **cup whipping cream**
    2/3 **cup packed brown sugar**
    2/3 **cup butter *or* margarine**
    1 **cup (6 ounces) semisweet chocolate chips**
    1 **cup chopped pecans**
Ice cream

In a saucepan over medium heat, bring cream, brown sugar and butter to a boil, stirring constantly. Reduce heat; simmer for 2 minutes, stirring occasionally. Remove from the heat; stir in the chocolate chips until melted and smooth. Stir in pecans. Serve warm over ice cream. Store in the refrigerator. **Yield:** 3 cups.

Chocolate Malted Ice Cream

(Pictured on page 66)

As a child, I helped crank out gallons of homemade ice cream. And thanks to this recipe, I'm carrying on the tradition in my family. We're chocolate fans—so you can imagine the reaction when we spoon up this fudgy summer treat. —Rose Hare, Mountain Home, Idaho

    5 **eggs, beaten**
    1 **cup sugar**
  1/2 **cup chocolate malted milk powder**
    2 **cups milk**
    1 **tablespoon vanilla extract**
    4 **cups whipping cream**
    1 **cup malted milk balls, coarsely crushed**

In a heavy saucepan, combine the eggs, sugar and malted milk powder. Gradually add milk. Cook and stir over low heat until mixture reaches 160° and coats the back of a metal spoon. Remove from the heat. Cool quickly by placing pan in a bowl of ice water; stir for 2 minutes. Stir in vanilla. Press plastic wrap onto surface of custard.

Refrigerate the custard for several hours or overnight.

Stir in cream and malted milk balls. Fill cylinder of ice cream freezer two-thirds full; freeze according to manufacturer's instructions. Refrigerate remaining mixture until ready to freeze. Allow to ripen in ice cream freezer or firm up in your refrigerator freezer 2-4 hours before serving. **Yield:** 2 quarts.

Chocolate Peanut Ice Cream Dessert

(Pictured below)

If you're expecting company or simply want a convenient on-hand dessert, try this. It's easy, but people will think that you slaved for hours to make it. —Jeanette Neufeld
Boissevain, Manitoba

    1 **cup vanilla wafer crumbs**
  1/2 **cup finely chopped peanuts**
  1/4 **cup butter *or* margarine, melted**
    2 **tablespoons confectioners' sugar**
    6 **cups chocolate ice cream, softened, *divided***
FILLING:
    1 **package (3 ounces) cream cheese, softened**
  1/3 **cup crunchy peanut butter**
  3/4 **cup confectioners' sugar**
  1/4 **cup milk**
  1/2 **cup whipping cream, whipped**

Line the bottom and sides of a 9-in. x 5-in. x 3-in. loaf pan with heavy-duty aluminum foil. Combine the first four ingredients; press half onto the bottom of the pan. Freeze for 15 minutes. Spread half of the ice cream over crust; freeze for 1 hour or until firm.

Meanwhile, for filling, beat cream cheese and peanut butter in a mixing bowl. Add sugar and milk; mix well. Fold in whipped cream. Spread over ice cream; freeze for 1 hour or until firm. Spread with remaining ice cream (pan will be very full). Press remaining crumb mixture on top. Cover and freeze for several hours or overnight.

Remove from the freezer 10 minutes before serving. Using foil, remove loaf from pan; discard foil. Cut into slices using a serrated knife. **Yield:** 10-12 servings.

Chocolate Mint Ice Cream

(Pictured above)

When the weather gets hot, my family really enjoys this cool combination of chocolate and mint. It doesn't require an ice cream maker—all that you need is an ordinary freezer. My ice cream's versatile, too. We've used crushed Heath bars, Oreo cookies and miniature chocolate chips in place of the Andes candies.   —Fran Skaff, Egg Harbor, Wisconsin

    1 can (14 ounces) sweetened condensed milk
    1/2 cup chocolate syrup
    2 cups whipping cream
    1 package (4.67 ounces) mint Andes candies (28
      pieces), chopped

In a small bowl, combine the milk and chocolate syrup; set aside. In a mixing bowl, beat cream until stiff peaks form. Fold in chocolate mixture and candies. Transfer to a freezer-proof container; cover and freeze for 5 hours or until firm. Remove from the freezer 10 minutes before serving. **Yield:** 1-1/2 quarts.

Heavenly Fudge Sauce

My fudge sauce is an all-purpose topping. It's so good, I've even given it as a special fresh-from-the-kitchen Christmas present to friends.   —Jane Payne
Twin Falls, Idaho

    1 square (1 ounce) unsweetened chocolate
    1/4 cup butter (no substitutes)
    1-1/2 cups confectioners' sugar
    1/4 teaspoon salt
    1/3 cup evaporated milk
Sliced bananas, orange sections *or* cubed angel food
  cake

Melt chocolate and butter in a small saucepan over very low heat. Whisk in sugar and salt alternately with milk; bring just to a boil over medium-low heat, stirring constantly. Serve warm over bananas, oranges or cake. Store in the refrigerator. **Yield:** 4-6 servings (1 cup).

Frozen Chocolate Torte

This cool make-ahead dessert is one of my favorites, especially in summer. —Tammy Neubauer, Ida Grove, Iowa

    1 package (10-1/2 ounces) miniature
      marshmallows
    1 cup (6 ounces) semisweet chocolate chips
    1 can (12 ounces) evaporated milk
    1 cup flaked coconut
    1/2 cup butter *or* margarine
    2 cups graham cracker crumbs
    1/2 gallon vanilla ice cream, softened

In a saucepan over low heat, melt marshmallows and chocolate chips with milk. Remove from heat; cool. In a skillet, stir coconut in butter until browned. Remove from heat; stir in crumbs. Pat three-fourths into a 13-in. x 9-in. x 2-in. baking pan; cool.

Spoon half of the ice cream onto crust. Top with half of the chocolate mixture. Layer with remaining ice cream and chocolate. Sprinkle with remaining crumbs. Cover; freeze for 2 hours. **Yield:** 12 servings.

Rocky Road Freeze

(Pictured below)

In place of peanuts, try using walnuts, pecans or cashews. Or substitute peanut butter chips for the chocolate chips.
—Sheila Berry, Carrying Place, Ontario

    1 can (14 ounces) sweetened condensed milk
    1/2 cup chocolate syrup
    2 cups whipping cream
    1 cup miniature marshmallows
    1/2 cup miniature chocolate chips
    1/2 cup chopped salted peanuts

In a small bowl, combine the milk and chocolate syrup; set aside. In a mixing bowl, beat cream until stiff peaks form. Fold in chocolate mixture, marshmallows, chocolate chips and peanuts. Transfer to a freezer-proof container; cover and freeze for 5 hours or until firm. Remove from freezer 10 minutes before serving. **Yield:** about 1-1/2 quarts.

Chocolate Pudding Sundaes

(Pictured at right)

This smooth microwave pudding tastes great over ice cream. It's easy to fix when our grandchildren pop in.
—Ruth Peterson, Jenison, Michigan

    2/3 cup sugar
    1/4 cup baking cocoa
      3 tablespoons cornstarch
    1/4 teaspoon salt
    2-1/4 cups milk
      2 tablespoons butter *or* margarine
      1 teaspoon vanilla extract
      3 cups vanilla ice cream

In a microwave-safe bowl, combine sugar, cocoa, cornstarch and salt. Gradually stir in milk until smooth. Microwave, uncovered, on high for 7-10 minutes, stirring every 2 minutes, until sauce comes to a boil. Stir in butter and vanilla. Serve warm over ice cream. Store in the refrigerator. **Yield:** 6 servings.

   Editor's Note: This recipe was tested in an 850-watt microwave.

Brownie Caramel Parfaits

(Pictured below)

Layers of toasted coconut and nuts add nice crunch and make this dessert seem fancy. But it really couldn't be simpler to put together. *—Chris Schnittka*
Charlottesville, Virginia

    1/2 cup chopped pecans
    1/2 cup shredded coconut
      1 package brownie mix (8-inch x 8-inch pan size)
      1 pint vanilla ice cream
      1 jar (12-1/4 ounces) caramel ice cream topping

Place pecans and coconut in an ungreased baking pan. Bake at 350° for 10-12 minutes or until toasted, stirring frequently. Meanwhile, prepare brownies according to package directions. Cool; cut into small squares. When ready to serve, layer the brownies, ice cream, caramel topping and pecan mixture in parfait or dessert glasses; repeat layers one or two times. **Yield:** 6 servings.

   Editor's Note: Any type of nuts, ice cream or topping may be used in these parfaits.

Chocolate Mint Dessert

(Pictured on page 66)

A rich fudge layer plus nuts and coconut make this dessert perfect for when you want to serve something special without last-minute fuss. It's easy to make the day before and freeze overnight. *—Barb Seibenaler*
Random Lake, Wisconsin

      1 cup butter (no substitutes), *divided*
      1 package (10 ounces) flaked coconut
    1/4 cup packed brown sugar
    1/4 cup chopped pecans
      4 squares (1 ounce *each*) unsweetened chocolate
    1-1/2 cups sugar
      1 can (12 ounces) evaporated milk
      1 teaspoon vanilla extract
      2 quarts mint chocolate chip ice cream, softened

In a skillet, melt 1/2 cup butter. Add coconut; cook and stir until golden brown. Remove from the heat. Stir in brown sugar and pecans; mix well. Set aside 1 cup. Press remaining coconut mixture onto the bottom and up the sides of a greased 13-in. x 9-in. x 2-in. dish.

   In a saucepan over medium heat, melt the chocolate and remaining butter. Add sugar and milk. Bring to a slow boil; cook for 5 minutes. Remove from the heat; stir in vanilla. Cool; pour over coconut mixture. Spread ice cream over top. Sprinkle with the reserved coconut mixture. Freeze for 6-8 hours or overnight. Remove from the freezer 15 minutes before serving. The dessert may be frozen for up to 2 months. **Yield:** 16-20 servings.

German Chocolate Ice Cream

(Pictured on page 66)

I found this recipe years ago and have been taking it to ice cream socials ever since. But you won't want to wait for a get-together to enjoy it. The cool combination of chocolate, coconut and pecans is delicious anytime.

—Peggy Key, Grant, Alabama

1-1/2 cups sugar
1/4 cup all-purpose flour
1/4 teaspoon ground cinnamon
1/4 teaspoon salt
4 cups milk
3 eggs, beaten
1 quart half-and-half cream
2 packages (4 ounces *each*) German sweet chocolate, melted
1 cup flaked coconut
1 cup chopped pecans

In a large heavy saucepan, combine the sugar, flour, cinnamon and salt. Gradually add milk and eggs; stir until smooth. Cook and stir over medium-low heat until mixture is thick enough to coat a metal spoon and reaches 160°, about 15 minutes. Stir in the remaining ingredients. Refrigerate for several hours or overnight.

Fill ice cream freezer cylinder two-thirds full; freeze according to manufacturer's instructions. Refrigerate remaining mixture until ready to freeze. Remove ice cream from the freezer 10 minutes before serving. **Yield:** 1 gallon.

Crunchy Chocolate Sauce

(Pictured below)

I dress up ice cream with an easy three-ingredient topping that's full of nuts. As this rich chocolate sauce cools over the ice cream, it forms a hard shell that kids (and adults) love. —Dolores Kastello, Waukesha, Wisconsin

1 cup chopped walnuts *or* pecans
1/2 cup butter (no substitutes)
1 cup (6 ounces) semisweet chocolate chips
Ice cream

In a skillet, saute nuts in butter until golden. Remove from the heat; stir in chocolate chips until melted. Serve warm over ice cream (sauce will harden). Store in the refrigerator. This sauce can be reheated in the microwave. **Yield:** about 1-1/2 cups.

Caramel Fudge Sundaes

(Pictured above)

I usually keep a supply of this sauce in the refrigerator at all times so I can make one of these sundaes whenever I crave one. The recipe has wonderful chocolate-caramel flavor and has been in our family for years. —Auton Miller, Piney Flats, Tennessee

1 can (12 ounces) evaporated milk
1 cup sugar
Dash salt
1 cup butter *or* margarine
3 tablespoons dark corn syrup
1 cup (6 ounces) semisweet chocolate chips
24 caramels
1/2 teaspoon vanilla extract
Vanilla ice cream
Chopped pecans *or* peanuts, optional

In a saucepan, combine the first seven ingredients. Cook, stirring constantly, over medium heat until the caramels are melted and mixture is smooth (do not boil). Reduce heat to low. With an electric hand mixer on medium speed, beat in vanilla; continue beating for 5 minutes. Beat on high for 2 minutes. Remove from the heat and cool for 30 minutes (sauce will thicken as it cools).

Serve over ice cream; sprinkle with nuts if desired. Reheat in the top of a double boiler over simmering water. Store in the refrigerator. **Yield:** 1 quart sauce.

Ice Cream Sandwich Dessert

(Pictured above)

No one will believe this awesome dessert is just dressed-up ice cream sandwiches. For my son's birthday party, I decorated it with race cars and checkered flags because he's a big racing fan. It was a huge success! —Jody Koerber
Caledonia, Wisconsin

  19 ice cream sandwiches
  1 carton (12 ounces) frozen whipped topping, thawed
  1 jar (11-3/4 ounces) hot fudge ice cream topping
  1 cup salted peanuts

Cut one ice cream sandwich in half. Place one whole and one half sandwich along a short side of an ungreased 13-in. x 9-in. x 2-in. pan. Arrange eight sandwiches in opposite direction in the pan. Spread with half of the whipped topping. Spoon fudge topping by teaspoonfuls onto whipped topping. Sprinkle with 1/2 cup peanuts.

Repeat layers with remaining ice cream sandwiches, whipped topping and peanuts (pan will be full). Cover and freeze for up to 2 months. Remove from the freezer 20 minutes before serving. Cut into squares. **Yield:** 12-15 servings.

Sweetheart Brownie Sundae

(Pictured on page 66)

I make this special treat for my family whenever there's a birthday or anniversary. Even without a special occasion, it caps any meal with a festive flair. I especially like to prepare the brownies in a heart shape for Valentine's Day and garnish them with berries. —Dottie Miller
Jonesborough, Tennessee

  1/4 cup butter (no substitutes)
  2 squares (1 ounce *each*) semisweet chocolate
  1 egg

  1/2 cup packed brown sugar
  1 teaspoon vanilla extract
  1/4 teaspoon salt
  1/4 cup all-purpose flour
  1 cup vanilla ice cream, softened
CHOCOLATE SAUCE:
  1 cup water
  1/2 cup baking cocoa
  1/4 cup sugar
  2 tablespoons butter
Confectioners' sugar

In a microwave oven or double boiler, melt butter and chocolate; cool for 10 minutes. In a mixing bowl, beat egg, brown sugar, vanilla and salt. Stir in chocolate mixture. Add flour; mix well. Line an 8-in. square baking pan with foil and grease the foil. Spread batter evenly into pan (batter will be thin). Bake at 350° for 15 minutes or until a toothpick inserted near the center comes out clean.

Cool completely on a wire rack. Cover and refrigerate until firm. Using a 3-1/2-in. x 3-1/2-in. heart pattern or cookie cutter, mark four hearts on surface of brownies; cut with a knife. Spread ice cream on two hearts; top each with a second heart. Wrap in plastic wrap; freeze in a single layer overnight.

For chocolate sauce, combine water, cocoa and sugar in a saucepan; bring to a boil over medium heat, stirring constantly. Reduce heat; simmer for 2-3 minutes or until thickened. Remove from the heat; stir in butter until melted. To serve, dust brownie hearts with confectioners' sugar and drizzle with warm chocolate sauce. Store any leftover sauce in the refrigerator. **Yield:** 2 servings.

Chocolate Dessert Cups

(Pictured below)

This elegant party dessert is tailor-made for Christmas. Making the chocolate cups is a bit time-consuming—but they look so pretty, they're worth the effort. —Ellen Govertsen, Wheaton, Illinois

1 cup (6 ounces) semisweet chocolate chips
1 tablespoon shortening
8 scoops peppermint ice cream
Miniature candy canes

In a microwave oven or saucepan, melt the chocolate chips and shortening. Brush evenly on the inside of eight paper or foil muffin cup liners. Chill until hardened, about 25 minutes. Remove liners. Fill chocolate cups with ice cream. Garnish with candy canes. **Yield:** 8 servings.

Mint Chip Ice Cream

(Pictured below)

We have a milk cow, so homemade ice cream has become a regular treat for our family. This version is very creamy with a mild mint flavor that goes well with the mini chocolate chips. It was an instant hit with my husband and our two little girls.   —Farrah McGuire, Springdale, Washington

   3 eggs, lightly beaten
1-3/4 cups milk
   3/4 cup sugar
Pinch salt
1-3/4 cups whipping cream
   1 teaspoon vanilla extract
   1/4 teaspoon peppermint extract
   4 drops green food coloring, optional
   1/2 cup miniature semisweet chocolate chips

In a saucepan, combine the eggs, milk, sugar and salt. Cook and stir over medium heat until mixture reaches 160° and coats a metal spoon. Cool to room temperature. Stir in cream, vanilla, peppermint extract and food coloring if desired. Refrigerate for 2 hours.

Stir in the chocolate chips. Fill ice cream freezer cylinder two-thirds full; freeze according to the manufacturer's directions. Refrigerate remaining mixture until ready to freeze. **Yield:** 1-1/2 quarts.

Chocolate Sauce

(Pictured above)

I make different toppings so we can enjoy our favorite snack—ice cream. This smooth chocolate sauce is always a bit hit.   —Nancy McDonald, Burns, Wyoming

   1/2 cup butter (no substitutes)
   2 squares (1 ounce *each*) unsweetened chocolate
   2 cups sugar
   1 cup half-and-half cream *or* evaporated milk
   1/2 cup light corn syrup
   1 teaspoon vanilla extract

In a saucepan, melt butter and chocolate. Add sugar, cream, corn syrup and vanilla. Bring to a boil, stirring constantly. Boil for 1-1/2 minutes. Remove from the heat. Serve warm or cold over ice cream or pound cake. Store in the refrigerator. **Yield:** about 3-1/3 cups.

German Chocolate Sundaes

This terrific topping is a real treat over chocolate ice cream. It's fun and fancy at the same time and much cooler to make on hot days than a German chocolate cake.
   —DeEtta Rasmussen, Fort Madison, Iowa

   1/2 cup sugar
   1/2 cup evaporated milk
   1/4 cup butter *or* margarine
   2 egg yolks, beaten
   2/3 cup flaked coconut
   1/2 cup chopped pecans
   1 teaspoon vanilla extract
Chocolate ice cream
Chocolate syrup, toasted coconut and additional chopped pecans, optional

In a heavy saucepan, combine the sugar, milk, butter and egg yolks. Bring to a boil over medium heat, stirring constantly; cook and stir for 2 minutes or until thickened. Remove from the heat. Stir in the coconut, pecans and vanilla. Stir until sauce is cooled slightly. Serve over ice cream. Top with chocolate syrup, coconut and pecans if desired. Store in the refrigerator. **Yield:** 1-1/4 cups.

RASPBERRY WHITE CHOCOLATE MOUSSE,
PAGE 83

MINTY COCOA MOUSSE,
PAGE 79

CHOCOLATE BERRY PARFAITS,
PAGE 80

CHOCOLATE TRUFFLE PIE, PAGE 76

Pies, Pudding & Mousse

White Chocolate Pie

(Pictured above)

For Valentine's Day, tint whipped topping pink to cover this creamy dessert. Sprinkle the pie with a crushed Heath candy bar, or garnish each slice with an Oreo cookie for a fast finishing touch. —Sue Brown, Hanover, Indiana

1 package (8 ounces) cream cheese, softened
3/4 cup confectioners' sugar
1 carton (8 ounces) frozen whipped topping, thawed, *divided*
1 chocolate crumb crust (8 inches)
1-1/4 cups cold milk
1 package (3.3 ounces) instant white chocolate pudding mix
Red food coloring

In a mixing bowl, beat cream cheese, confectioners' sugar and 1/4 cup whipped topping until light and fluffy. Spread over crust. In a mixing bowl, beat milk and pudding mix on low speed for 2 minutes. Pour over cream cheese mixture. Refrigerate for 2 hours or until firm.

Tint remaining whipped topping pink with red food coloring. Spread over pie just before serving. Refrigerate leftovers. **Yield:** 6-8 servings.

Rich Chocolate Pudding

(Pictured at right)

Creamy, smooth and fudgy, this dessert is a true chocolate indulgence. With just four ingredients, it might be the easiest from-scratch pudding you'll ever make. But it's so delicious and elegant looking, your guests will think you spent hours stirring it up. —Verna Hainer
Aurora, Colorado

2 cups (12 ounces) semisweet chocolate chips
1/3 cup confectioners' sugar
1 cup milk
1/4 cup butter *or* margarine
Whipped topping and miniature semisweet chocolate chips, optional

Place chocolate chips and confectioners' sugar in a blender; cover and process until the chips are coarsely chopped. In a saucepan over medium heat, bring milk and butter to a boil. Add to blender; cover and process

until chips are melted and mixture is smooth.

Pour into six individual serving dishes. Refrigerate. Garnish with whipped topping and miniature chips if desired. **Yield:** 6 servings.

Chocolate Truffle Pie

(Pictured on page 74)

Warm days warrant a cool dessert like this frosty and refreshing pie. The raspberry sauce combined with rich chocolate and ice cream make each slice irresistible. All eyes will light up when you pull out this pleaser! —Mercelle Jackson, Rochester, New York

1 cup chocolate wafer crumbs
1/4 cup butter *or* margarine, melted
1 pint chocolate ice cream, softened
1 cup (6 ounces) semisweet chocolate chips
1/3 cup whipping cream
1 pint vanilla ice cream, softened
2 tablespoons slivered almonds, toasted
1 package (10 ounces) frozen sweetened raspberries, thawed
1 tablespoon cornstarch

In a bowl, combine wafer crumbs and butter. Press onto the bottom and up the sides of a 9-in. pie plate coated with nonstick cooking spray. Freeze for 30 minutes. Spread chocolate ice cream over crust; freeze for 1 hour or until firm.

In a microwave oven or small saucepan, heat chocolate chips and whipping cream until chips are melted; stir until smooth. Cool slightly. Quickly and carefully spread over chocolate ice cream. Freeze for 30 minutes. Top with vanilla ice cream; sprinkle with almonds. Cover and freeze until firm.

For sauce, puree the raspberries in a blender or food processor until smooth. Strain and discard seeds. In a saucepan, combine cornstarch and raspberry juice until smooth. Bring to a boil; cook and stir for 1-2 minutes or until thickened. Cool completely. Remove pie from the freezer 10 minutes before cutting. Serve over raspberry sauce. **Yield:** 8 servings.

Chocolate Mallow Pie

(Pictured above)

This rich and fudgy cream cheese pie should serve eight, but it never does because so many folks request a second slice! I've been cooking for more than 60 years...and this is the best chocolate pie recipe I've found. —Louise Genn
Cosmopolis, Washington

1-1/4 cups crushed cream-filled chocolate sandwich
     cookies (about 14 cookies)
  1/4 cup butter *or* margarine, melted
    2 tablespoons sugar
    2 packages (one 8 ounces, one 3 ounces) cream
     cheese, softened
  1/2 cup chocolate syrup
1-1/3 cups semisweet chocolate chips, melted
    1 carton (8 ounces) frozen whipped topping,
     thawed
    2 cups miniature marshmallows
Chocolate curls, optional

In a bowl, combine the cookie crumbs, butter and sugar. Press onto the bottom and up the sides of a 9-in. pie plate. Bake at 375° for 8-10 minutes or until set; cool completely on a wire rack.

   In a mixing bowl, beat cream cheese and chocolate syrup until blended. Beat in melted chips. Set aside 1/4 cup of whipped topping. Fold marshmallows and remaining whipped topping into chocolate mixture. Spoon into crust. Refrigerate for at least 8 hours or overnight. Garnish with reserved whipped topping and chocolate curls if desired. **Yield:** 8 servings.

Sweetheart Fudge Pie

If your sweetie is a chocolate fan, this pie is a perfect way to declare your devotion—on Valentine's Day or any time of the year! —Kim Marie Van Rheenen, Mendota, Illinois

    1 unbaked pastry shell (9 inches)
  1/4 cup butter *or* margarine, softened
  3/4 cup packed brown sugar
    3 eggs

    2 cups (12 ounces) semisweet chocolate chips,
     melted
    2 teaspoons instant coffee granules
  1/4 teaspoon vanilla *or* rum extract
    1 cup coarsely chopped walnuts
  1/4 cup all-purpose flour
    1 cup whipping cream
    2 tablespoons confectioners' sugar
    3 tablespoons chopped red maraschino cherries

Line pastry shell with a double thickness of heavy-duty foil. Bake at 450° for 5 minutes. Remove foil; set crust aside. In a small mixing bowl, cream butter and brown sugar. Add eggs, one at a time, beating well after each addition. Add chocolate, coffee and extract. Stir in walnuts and flour. Pour into crust. Bake at 375° for 28-30 minutes. Cool completely.

   In a small mixing bowl, beat cream and confectioners' sugar until stiff peaks form; fold in cherries. Spread over pie. **Yield:** 12-14 servings.

Chocolate Peppermint Pie

(Pictured below)

This delightful dessert will satisfy a chocolate lover's craving. It's quite simple as well. —Kristine Dorazio
Chepachet, Rhode Island

    1 quart chocolate-chocolate chip ice cream,
     softened
    1 chocolate cookie crust (9 inches)
    1 package (6 ounces) chocolate-covered
     peppermint candies
    1 cup whipping cream, *divided*

Spoon ice cream into crust. Freeze until firm, about 2 hours. Meanwhile, in a small saucepan, heat candies with 3-4 tablespoons of cream; stir until smooth. Cool. Whip the remaining cream; spoon over ice cream. Drizzle with some of the chocolate-peppermint sauce; pass the remaining sauce. **Yield:** 6-8 servings.

Chocolate Cream Pie

(Pictured at right)

Our teenage son, John, has done lots of 4-H baking. His favorite is this old-fashioned creamy chocolate pudding in a flaky crust. —Mary Anderson
De Valls Bluff, Arkansas

1-1/2 cups sugar
  1/3 cup all-purpose flour
    3 tablespoons baking cocoa
  1/2 teaspoon salt
1-1/2 cups water
    1 can (12 ounces) evaporated milk
    5 egg yolks, beaten
  1/2 cup butter *or* margarine
    1 teaspoon vanilla extract
    1 pastry shell (9 inches), baked
Whipped topping

In a large saucepan, combine the first six ingredients until smooth. Cook and stir over medium-high heat until thickened and bubbly, about 2 minutes. Reduce heat; cook and stir 2 minutes longer. Remove from the heat.

Stir 1 cup hot mixture into egg yolks. Return all to the pan; bring to a gentle boil, stirring constantly. Remove from the heat; stir in butter and vanilla. Cool slightly. Pour warm filling into pastry shell. Cool for 1 hour. Refrigerate until set. Just before serving, garnish with whipped topping. **Yield:** 6-8 servings.

Chocolate Cherry Pie

(Pictured below)

This rich and creamy pie is sure to please any dyed-in-the-wool chocoholic! —Maxine Smith
Owanka, South Dakota

    1 cup all-purpose flour
    2 tablespoons sugar
  1/2 teaspoon salt
  1/2 cup cold butter *or* margarine
FILLING:
    1 can (14 ounces) sweetened condensed milk
    1 cup (6 ounces) semisweet chocolate chips
  1/2 teaspoon salt
    1 can (21 ounces) cherry pie filling
  1/4 to 1/2 teaspoon almond extract
Whipped cream and maraschino cherries, optional

In a bowl, mix flour, sugar and salt. Cut in butter until mixture resembles coarse crumbs. Press firmly onto the bottom and sides of a 9-in. pie plate. Bake at 350° for 15-20 minutes or until golden brown. Cool completely.

In a saucepan, combine milk, chocolate chips and salt; cook and stir over low heat until chocolate melts. Stir in pie filling and extract. Pour into crust. Chill 2-3 hours or until firm. Garnish with whipped cream and cherries if desired. **Yield:** 8 servings.

Cool 'n' Creamy Chocolate Pie

My mother-in-law fixed this pie often for family get-togethers. It's one of my husband's favorite desserts. My two sons love it as well. —Christie Pyle, Owasso, Oklahoma

1-1/2 cups milk
    1 package (3.9 ounces) instant chocolate pudding mix
    1 package (3 ounces) cream cheese, softened
    1 cup confectioners' sugar
    1 carton (8 ounces) frozen whipped topping, thawed, *divided*
    1 chocolate crumb crust (8 *or* 9 inches)
    1 milk chocolate candy bar (1.55 ounces), chopped

In a mixing bowl, beat milk and pudding mix on low speed for 2 minutes or until thickened; set aside. In another mixing bowl, beat the cream cheese and confectioners' sugar until blended. Mix in 1 cup whipped topping. Spread into crust. Top with pudding mixture and remaining whipped topping. Sprinkle with chopped candy bar. Cover and refrigerate overnight. **Yield:** 8 servings.

Brownie Pie a la Mode

(Pictured at right)

This is a quick recipe for when you need something good and chocolaty. Cutting brownies into wedges and topping them with fudge sauce makes a heavenly dessert.
—Beverly Thornton, Cortlandt Manor, New York

1/2 cup sugar
2 tablespoons butter *or* margarine
2 tablespoons water
1-1/2 cups semisweet chocolate chips
2 eggs
1 teaspoon vanilla extract
2/3 cup all-purpose flour
1/4 teaspoon baking soda
1/4 teaspoon salt
3/4 cup chopped walnuts
FUDGE SAUCE:
1 cup (6 ounces) semisweet chocolate chips
1/2 cup evaporated milk
1/4 cup sugar
1 tablespoon butter *or* margarine
Vanilla ice cream

In a small saucepan over medium heat, bring sugar, butter and water to a boil. Remove from the heat; stir in chocolate chips until melted. In a mixing bowl, beat eggs and vanilla. Add chocolate mixture; mix well. Combine flour, baking soda and salt; add to chocolate mixture. Stir in walnuts. Pour into a greased 9-in. pie plate. Bake at 350° for 28-30 minutes or until a toothpick inserted near the center comes out clean. Cool on a wire rack.

For fudge sauce, heat chocolate chips, milk, sugar and butter in a microwave oven or double boiler until chocolate and butter are melted; stir until smooth. Drizzle some over pie. Cut into wedges; serve with ice cream and additional sauce. **Yield:** 6-8 servings.

1-1/2 cups cold milk
1 package (3.9 ounces) instant chocolate pudding mix
1 carton (8 ounces) frozen whipped topping, thawed
1 cup (6 ounces) semisweet chocolate chips
1 cup miniature marshmallows, *divided*
1/2 cup salted peanuts
1/4 cup chocolate syrup, optional

In a mixing bowl, beat milk and pudding mix on low speed for 2 minutes. Fold in the whipped topping, chocolate chips, 3/4 cup marshmallows and peanuts. Pour into dessert dishes. Refrigerate until serving. Sprinkle with remaining marshmallows; drizzle with chocolate syrup if desired. **Yield:** 8 servings.

Minty Cocoa Mousse

(Pictured on page 74)

Junior Mints give the refreshing mint taste to this scrumptious smooth-as-silk mousse. It's one of my best desserts because it's a snap to prepare, yet the flavor is beyond compare.
—Melissa Tarbox, Allen, Texas

2 tablespoons baking cocoa
2 tablespoons milk
1 cup Junior Mints
2 tablespoons butter *or* margarine
1 carton (8 ounces) frozen whipped topping, thawed, *divided*
1/2 teaspoon vanilla extract
Fresh mint and additional whipped topping, optional

In a saucepan, combine cocoa and milk until smooth. Add mints and butter; cook and stir over low heat until smooth. Cool for 15 minutes. Stir in 1 cup whipped topping and vanilla. Fold in the remaining whipped topping. Spoon into dessert dishes. Refrigerate until serving. Garnish with mint and whipped topping if desired. **Yield:** 4 servings.

Rocky Road Pudding

(Pictured below)

Our daughters love chocolate, so this light fluffy dessert is a delightful way to satisfy their taste buds.
—Tracy Golder, Bloomsburg, Pennsylvania

Chocolate 'n' Toffee Rice Pudding

(Pictured above)

I can't think of a more comforting dessert than this pudding. The toffee bits add a crunch to its creamy consistency. It looks especially pretty layered in a parfait glass.
—JoAnn Vess Hilliard, East Liverpool, Ohio

    3 cups milk
    3 cups cooked rice
1/2 cup packed brown sugar
    3 tablespoons butter *or* margarine
1/4 teaspoon salt
    1 teaspoon vanilla extract
1/4 cup flaked coconut, toasted
1/4 cup English toffee bits *or* almond brickle chips
1/4 cup miniature semisweet chocolate chips
1/2 cup whipped topping
    7 maraschino cherries

In a large saucepan, combine the milk, rice, brown sugar, butter and salt; bring to a boil over medium heat. Cook for 15 minutes or until thick and creamy, stirring occasionally. Remove from the heat; stir in vanilla. Cool.

Spoon half of the pudding into dessert dishes. Combine the coconut, toffee bits and chocolate chips; sprinkle half over the pudding. Repeat layers. Refrigerate until serving. Garnish with the whipped topping and cherries. **Yield:** 7 servings.

Chocolate Berry Parfaits

(Pictured on page 74)

This luscious dessert is easy to make for weekday dinners, yet pretty enough for company. Instant chocolate pudding is layered with a mixture of pureed strawberries and whipped cream to create yummy parfaits.

—Lynn McAllister
Mount Ulla, North Carolina

    2 cups cold milk
    1 package (3.9 ounces) instant chocolate pudding mix
    1 package (10 ounces) frozen sweetened strawberries, thawed
    1 cup whipping cream
1/4 cup confectioners' sugar
Sliced fresh strawberries, optional

In a mixing bowl, beat milk and pudding mix until thick and smooth, about 2 minutes; set aside. Drain strawberries (discard the juice or save for another use); place berries in a blender. Cover and process until smooth; set aside. In a mixing bowl, beat cream and sugar until stiff peaks form. Gently fold in strawberry puree.

Divide half of the chocolate pudding among four or six parfait glasses or bowls. Top with half of the strawberry mixture. Repeat layers. Garnish with a strawberry slice if desired. **Yield:** 4-6 servings.

Editor's Note: 2 cups of whipped topping may be substituted for the whipping cream and sugar.

Chocolate Mint Parfaits

(Pictured below)

This minty chocolate pudding dessert tastes so light and refreshing. —Karalee Reinke, Omaha, Nebraska

    2 cups plus 1 tablespoon cold milk, *divided*
    1 package (3.9 ounces) instant chocolate pudding mix
    4 ounces cream cheese, softened
    1 tablespoon sugar
1/4 teaspoon peppermint extract
    1 cup whipped topping
    4 to 6 mint Andes candies, optional

In a bowl, whisk 2 cups milk and pudding mix for 2 minutes; set aside. In a small mixing bowl, beat cream cheese, sugar, extract and remaining milk. Fold in whipped topping. In parfait or dessert glasses, layer the pudding and cream cheese mixtures. Garnish with mint candies if desired. **Yield:** 4-6 servings.

Chocolate Banana Cream Pie

(Pictured at right)

My husband loves banana cream pie, and I like chocolate, so I combined the two. It's our favorite dessert, which means I get a lot of practice making it!
—Jaquelin McTee, Eatonville, Washington

1/2 cup sugar
1/4 cup cornstarch
1/4 teaspoon salt
1-1/2 cups milk
   1 cup whipping cream
   3 egg yolks, lightly beaten
   1 tablespoon butter *or* margarine
   2 teaspoons vanilla extract
   1 pastry shell (9 inches), baked
   4 squares (1 ounce *each*) semisweet
      chocolate, melted
   2 medium firm bananas, sliced
Whipped cream and chocolate shavings, optional

In a saucepan, combine sugar, cornstarch and salt. Gradually add milk and cream until smooth. Cook and stir over medium-high heat until thickened and bubbly, about 2 minutes. Add a small amount to egg yolks; mix well. Return all to the pan. Bring to a gentle boil; cook for 2 minutes, stirring constantly. Remove from the heat; stir in butter and vanilla.

   Pour half into the pastry shell; cover and refrigerate. Add chocolate to remaining custard; mix well. Cover and refrigerate for 1 hour. Do not stir. Arrange bananas over filling. Carefully spoon chocolate custard over all. Refrigerate for at least 2 hours. Garnish with whipped cream and chocolate shavings if desired. **Yield:** 6-8 servings.

Heavenly Chocolate Mousse

(Pictured below)

"Heaven on a spoon" is how one friend describes this chocolaty dessert. My husband, Allen, rates it best of all the special treats I've made. The filling can also be used for a pie. —Christy Freeman, Central Point, Oregon

   8 squares (1 ounce *each*) semisweet baking
      chocolate, coarsely chopped
1/2 cup water, *divided*
   2 tablespoons butter (no substitutes)
   3 egg yolks
   2 tablespoons sugar
1-1/4 cups whipping cream, whipped

In a microwave oven or double boiler, heat chocolate, 1/4 cup water and butter until the chocolate and butter are melted. Cool for 10 minutes. In a small heavy saucepan, whisk egg yolks, sugar and remaining water. Cook and stir over low heat until mixture reaches 160°, about 1-2 minutes. Remove from the heat; whisk in chocolate mixture.

   Set saucepan in ice and stir until cooled, about 5-10 minutes. Fold in whipped cream. Spoon into dessert dishes. Refrigerate for 4 hours or overnight. **Yield:** 6-8 servings.

Grandma's Chocolate Pudding

My grandmother always made this creamy, very chocolaty pudding when we visited. —Donna Hughes
Rochester, New Hampshire

   1 cup sugar
1/2 cup baking cocoa
1/4 cup all-purpose flour
   2 cups water
3/4 cup evaporated milk
   1 tablespoon vanilla extract
Pinch salt

In a saucepan, combine sugar, cocoa and flour. Add water and milk; stir until smooth. Cook over medium heat, stirring constantly, until mixture comes to a boil. Cook until thick, about 1 minute. Remove from heat; stir in vanilla and salt. Cool to room temperature, stirring several times. Pour into dessert dishes. Serve warm or chilled. **Yield:** 4-6 servings.

Chocolate Fudge Mousse

Instant pudding is the "secret ingredient" that makes this chocolate dessert such a breeze to prepare. It's so much quicker and easier to whip up than a traditional mousse. But it's equally fluffy and luscious, so it even satisfies my husband's rather large sweet tooth. —Carly Carter
Nashville, Tennessee

    2 cups cold milk
    1 package (3.9 ounces) instant chocolate
      pudding mix
    1/4 cup hot fudge ice cream topping
    3 cups whipped topping

In a mixing bowl, beat milk and pudding mix on low speed for 2 minutes. Stir in fudge topping. Fold in whipped topping until blended. Pour into dessert dishes. Chill until serving. **Yield:** 6 servings.

Banana Surprise

(Pictured below)

You can make the pudding more of a surprise by also adding whipped topping or fresh strawberries so that it's like a creamy banana split. —Jean Atherly
Red Lodge, Montana

    1/4 cup instant banana *or* chocolate drink mix
    4 cups cold milk
    2 packages (3.9 ounces *each*) instant chocolate
      pudding mix*
    4 medium bananas, sliced

In a medium bowl, combine drink mix and milk. Add pudding mix and beat according to package directions. Pour half into eight small bowls; top with banana slices and remaining pudding. **Yield:** 8 servings.
    *Editor's Note:** Vanilla or banana pudding can be substituted for the chocolate pudding.

Frosty Chocolate Mousse

(Pictured above)

This is a wonderful dessert that whips up fast. It's very smooth and silky and is a perfect complement to any meal. —Myra Innes, Auburn, Kansas

1-1/2 cups whipping cream
    1/2 cup sugar
    1/2 cup sifted baking cocoa
    1/2 teaspoon rum extract
    1/2 teaspoon vanilla extract

In a mixing bowl, combine all ingredients. Beat until mixture mounds softly. Spoon into dessert dishes. Freeze for at least 2 hours before serving. **Yield:** 4 servings.

Black Forest Mousse

If you like chocolate and cherries, you'll love this smooth, light dessert. Pantry staples such as instant pudding and canned pie filling make it quick to fix and inexpensive. —Deanna Richter, Elmore, Minnesota

    2 cups milk
    1 package (3.9 ounces) instant chocolate
      pudding mix
    1 can (21 ounces) cherry pie filling
    2 cups whipped topping

In a bowl, beat the milk and pudding mix for 2 minutes or until smooth. Let stand until slightly thickened, about 2 minutes. Stir in pie filling. Gently fold in whipped topping. Spoon into dessert dishes; refrigerate until serving. **Yield:** 8 servings.

White Chocolate Mousse

(Pictured at right)

This elegant, fluffy dessert is a feast for the eyes and palate. Since almost any fresh fruit may be used, it can grace special meals throughout the year. The recipe is easy to double if you are hosting a larger group.

—Susan Herbert, Aurora, Illinois

> 1 cup whipping cream
> 2 tablespoons sugar
> 1 package (3 ounces) cream cheese, softened
> 3 squares (1 ounce *each*) white baking chocolate, melted
> 2 cups blueberries, raspberries *or* strawberries
> Additional berries, optional

In a mixing bowl, beat cream until soft peaks form. Gradually add sugar, beating until stiff peaks form; set aside. In another mixing bowl, beat cream cheese until fluffy. Add chocolate and beat until smooth. Fold in whipped cream. Alternate layers of mousse and berries in parfait glasses, ending with mousse. Garnish with additional berries if desired. Serve immediately or refrigerate for up to 3 hours. **Yield:** 4-6 servings.

Raspberry White Chocolate Mousse

(Pictured on page 74)

Raspberry sauce is an appealing base for this fluffy white chocolate mousse. The treasured treat is surprisingly easy and a delightful change of pace from heavier cakes and pies.   *—Mary Lou Wayman, Salt Lake City, Utah*

> 1 package (10 ounces) sweetened frozen raspberries, thawed
> 2 tablespoons sugar
> 1 tablespoon orange juice concentrate
> 2 cups whipping cream

> 6 squares (1 ounce *each*) white baking chocolate
> 1 teaspoon vanilla extract
> 1/4 cup milk chocolate chips
> 1 teaspoon vegetable oil

In a blender, combine the raspberries, sugar and orange juice concentrate; cover and process until smooth. Press through a sieve; discard seeds. Refrigerate sauce.

In a saucepan over low heat, cook and stir cream and white chocolate until chocolate is melted. Stir in vanilla. Transfer to a mixing bowl. Cover and refrigerate for 6 hours or until thickened, stirring occasionally.

Beat cream mixture on high speed until light and fluffy, about 1-1/2 minutes (do not overbeat). Just before serving, melt chocolate chips and oil in a microwave oven or saucepan. Spoon 2 tablespoons of raspberry sauce on each plate. Pipe or spoon 1/2 cup chocolate mousse over sauce; drizzle with melted chocolate. Store leftovers in the refrigerator. **Yield:** 8 servings.

Chocolate Peanut Dream Pie

(Pictured at left)

I love the flavor of peanut butter cups, so I dreamed up this creamy, rich pie to serve to company. It's wonderfully simple to make and always gets rave reviews.

—Rosanne Marshall, Depew, New York

> 1 package (3.4 ounces) cook-and-serve chocolate pudding mix
> 1/2 cup creamy peanut butter
> 1 cup whipped topping
> 1 graham cracker crust (9 inches)
> Peanuts and additional whipped topping, optional

Prepare pudding according to package directions. Remove from the heat; whisk in peanut butter. Place pan in a bowl of ice water for 5 minutes, stirring occasionally. Fold in whipped topping. Pour into the crust. Cover and refrigerate for 1 hour or until set. Garnish with peanuts and whipped topping if desired. **Yield:** 6-8 servings.

Frozen Chocolate Mint Pie

(Pictured above)

This refreshing pie was featured at a small resort my family visited regularly as I was growing up. When I make it now, I relish compliments from tasters, along with fond memories of sunny days at the beach and good home cooking. —Jenny Falk, Sauk Rapids, Minnesota

    3 egg whites
1/4 teaspoon cream of tartar
    1 cup sugar
CHOCOLATE SAUCE:
    1/4 cup butter (no substitutes)
      1 square (1 ounce) unsweetened chocolate
    1 cup sugar
    3/4 cup evaporated milk
    1/2 teaspoon vanilla extract
    1/8 teaspoon peppermint extract
Dash salt
    2 cups vanilla ice cream, softened
1-1/3 cups whipping cream, whipped

In a mixing bowl, beat egg whites until foamy. Add cream of tartar; beat until soft peaks form. Gradually add sugar, 1 tablespoon at a time, beating until stiff glossy peaks form. Spread onto the bottom and up the sides of a greased and floured 9-in. deep-dish pie plate. Bake at 275° for 1 hour. Turn off oven and do not open door; let meringue cool completely inside the oven.

For chocolate sauce, in heavy saucepan, melt butter and chocolate; stir until smooth. Stir in sugar and evaporated milk. Cook over low heat for 45-60 minutes or until thickened, stirring occasionally. Remove from the heat; stir in extracts and salt. Cool to room temperature.

Spread ice cream into meringue crust. Fold whipped cream into cooled chocolate sauce. Spread over ice cream layer; freeze until firm. **Yield:** 8 servings.

Chocolate Cookie Mousse

I have family members who beg for this rich yummy dessert whenever I visit. It calls for just four ingredients, and it's handy to keep in the freezer for a special occasion. —Carol Mullaney, Pittsburgh, Pennsylvania

    1 package (16 ounces) cream-filled chocolate sandwich cookies, *divided*
    2 tablespoons milk
    2 cups whipping cream, *divided*
    2 cups (12 ounces) semisweet chocolate chips

Crush 16 cookies; sprinkle into an 8-in. square dish. Drizzle with milk. In a microwave-safe bowl, combine 2/3 cup cream and chocolate chips. Microwave, uncovered, on high for 1 minute. Stir; microwave 30-60 seconds longer or until chips are melted. Stir until smooth; cool to room temperature.

Meanwhile, in a mixing bowl, beat remaining cream until soft peaks form. Fold into chocolate mixture. Spread a third of the chocolate mixture over crushed cookies. Separate eight cookies; place over chocolate mixture. Repeat. Top with remaining chocolate mixture. Garnish with remaining whole cookies. Cover and freeze for up to 2 months. Thaw in the refrigerator for at least 3 hours before serving. **Yield:** 16 servings.

Editor's Note: This recipe was tested in an 850-watt microwave.

Chocolate-Caramel Supreme Pie

(Pictured below)

At a church fund-raiser, I purchased a pie-a-month package furnished by a local family. From among all the varieties they made, this one was the best, with its chocolate crust, creamy caramel filling and fluffy topping. —Diana Stewart, Oelwein, Iowa

30 caramels*
3 tablespoons butter *or* margarine
2 tablespoons water
1 chocolate crumb crust (9 inches)
1/2 cup chopped pecans, toasted
1 package (3 ounces) cream cheese, softened
1/3 cup confectioners' sugar
3/4 cup milk chocolate chips
3 tablespoons hot water
1 carton (8 ounces) frozen whipped topping, thawed
Chocolate hearts *or* curls, optional

In a saucepan, combine the caramels, butter and water. Cook and stir over medium heat until caramels are melted. Spread over crust; sprinkle with pecans. Refrigerate for 1 hour. In a mixing bowl, beat cream cheese and sugar; spread over the caramel layer. Refrigerate.

In a saucepan, melt chocolate chips with hot water over low heat; stir until smooth. Cool slightly. Fold in whipped topping. Spread over cream cheese layer. Garnish with chocolate hearts or curls if desired. Chill until serving. Refrigerate leftovers. **Yield:** 8 servings.

*Editor's Note:** This recipe was tested with Hershey caramels.

Frozen Chocolate Pie

(Pictured below)

When I serve this dessert to company, they often think it has ice cream in it. It does have a smooth texture like an ice cream pie. I've been making this recipe for years—it's a refreshing end to a meal anytime. —Bonnie Scott
McLouth, Kansas

1 package (3 ounces) cream cheese, softened
1/2 cup sugar
1 teaspoon vanilla extract
1/3 cup baking cocoa

1/3 cup milk
1 carton (8 ounces) frozen whipped topping, thawed
1 pie pastry (9 inches), baked
Chocolate curls *or* chips, optional

In a mixing bowl, beat cream cheese, sugar and vanilla until smooth. Add cocoa alternately with milk; mix well. Fold in whipped topping. Pour into pie shell. Freeze for 8 hours or overnight. If desired, garnish with chocolate curls or chips. **Yield:** 6-8 servings.

Orange Chocolate Mousse

(Pictured above)

This easy-to-make dessert is one of my favorites to serve. It looks so elegant, and the velvety texture, with a subtle hint of orange, always brings smile to those at the table. —Shirley Glaab, Hattiesburg, Mississippi

1 egg, beaten
1 egg yolk, beaten
2 tablespoons brown sugar
1/2 to 1 teaspoon grated orange peel
1/2 cup whipping cream
4-1/2 teaspoons orange juice
3 squares (1 ounce *each*) semisweet chocolate, melted
Whipped cream and orange peel strips, optional

In a saucepan, combine the first six ingredients until blended. Cook and stir over medium-low heat for 15 minutes or until the mixture is thickened and reaches at least 160°. Remove from the heat; stir in melted chocolate until smooth.

Pour into dessert dishes. Refrigerate for at least 2 hours or until serving. Garnish with whipped cream and orange peel if desired. **Yield:** 2 servings.

STRAWBERRY CHOCOLATE SHORTCAKE,
PAGE 92

CHOCOLATE PUDDING PIZZA,
PAGE 90

CREAMY CANDY BAR DESSERT,
PAGE 88

VALENTINE BERRIES AND CREAM, PAGE 94

Just Desserts

Chocolate Souffle

(Pictured above)

This recipe has been treasured and passed down in our family for years. It came from my Aunt Clara, whose cooking was a blend of her country and rural French roots. I can always depend on everyone being home to eat—and on time—whenever I make this for dessert. —Carol Ice
Burlingham, New York

> 2 squares (1 ounce *each*) unsweetened chocolate
> 1/4 cup butter (no substitutes)
> 5 tablespoons all-purpose flour
> 1/3 cup plus 1 teaspoon sugar, *divided*
> 1/4 teaspoon salt
> 1 cup milk
> 3 eggs, *separated*
> 1 teaspoon vanilla extract
> 1/4 teaspoon almond extract
> SAUCE:
> 1 cup whipping cream
> 1/4 cup confectioners' sugar
> 1/4 teaspoon vanilla extract
> Baking cocoa *or* ground cinnamon, optional

In the top of a double boiler over simmering water, melt chocolate and butter. In a bowl, combine flour, 1/3 cup sugar and salt. Add milk; stir into melted chocolate. Cook and stir until thickened, about 7 minutes. In a small bowl, beat egg yolks; add a small amount of hot mixture. Return all to pan. Remove from heat; add extracts. In a small mixing bowl, beat egg whites and remaining sugar until stiff peaks form. Fold into chocolate mixture.

Grease the bottom of a 1-1/2-qt. baking dish; add chocolate mixture. Place dish in a larger pan; add 1 in. of hot water to pan. Bake at 325° for 1 hour or until a knife inserted near the center comes out clean. Combine the first three sauce ingredients in a small mixing bowl; beat until soft peaks form. Serve souffle warm with a dollop of sauce. Sprinkle with cocoa or cinnamon if desired. **Yield:** 4-6 servings.

Creamy Candy Bar Dessert

(Pictured on page 86)

Here's a dessert you'll have a hard time resisting until the end of the meal. It's every bit as yummy as it looks. One taste and you'll be smiling like a kid in a candy store, no matter what age you are! —Kathy Kittell, Lenexa, Kansas

> 2 cups graham cracker crumbs (about 32 squares)
> 3 tablespoons sugar
> 1/2 cup butter *or* margarine, melted
> 1 jar (11-3/4 ounces) hot fudge ice cream topping
> FILLING:
> 1/2 cup cold milk
> 2 packages (3.4 ounces *each*) instant vanilla *or* chocolate pudding mix
> 2 cartons (16 ounces *each*) frozen whipped topping, thawed
> 6 to 7 Snickers candy bars (2.07 ounces *each*), chopped, *divided*

In a bowl, combine the crumbs and sugar; stir in butter. Press into an ungreased 13-in. x 9-in. x 2-in. dish. In a small saucepan, heat the fudge topping over low heat until warmed; pour evenly over crust. Cool.

In a mixing bowl, beat the milk, pudding mix and whipped topping for 2-3 minutes or until stiff, scraping sides of bowl often. Stir in three-fourths of the candy bar pieces. Pour over crust. Sprinkle with remaining candy bar pieces. Cover and refrigerate for 2-3 hours or overnight. Refrigerate leftovers. **Yield:** 15 servings.

Chocolate Caramel Pears

(Pictured below)

Bring out a tray of these fancy fruit treats and watch everybody's eyes widen. The pears wear a nut-dusted caramel coating and an elegant drizzle of chocolate.
—Lisa Roberts, Grafton, Wisconsin

> 1 package (14 ounces) caramels*
> 2 tablespoons water
> 6 large firm pears with stems
> 1 cup chopped cashews, hazelnuts *or* almonds
> 1/3 cup semisweet chocolate chips

Black Forest Crepes

(Pictured below)

These fancy-looking crepes are a sweet ending to a special-occasion meal. I fill them with cherry pie filling and top them with chocolate sauce, whipped cream and a sprinkling of baking cocoa.
— Lisa Tanner
Warner Robins, Georgia

1-1/4 cups buttermilk
   3 eggs
   3 tablespoons butter *or* **margarine, melted**
   1 cup all-purpose flour
   2 tablespoons sugar
   2 tablespoons baking cocoa
CHOCOLATE SAUCE:
   3/4 cup sugar
   1/3 cup baking cocoa
   1 can (5 ounces) evaporated milk
   1/4 cup butter *or* **margarine**
   1 teaspoon vanilla extract
   1 can (21 ounces) cherry pie filling

In a bowl, combine buttermilk, eggs and butter. Combine flour, sugar and cocoa; add to milk mixture and mix well. Cover and chill for 1 hour. Heat a lightly greased 8-in. nonstick skillet; add 2 tablespoons batter. Lift and tilt pan to evenly coat bottom. Cook until top appears dry; turn and cook 15-20 seconds longer. Remove to a wire rack. Repeat with remaining batter. When cool, stack crepes with waxed paper or paper towels in between.

For sauce, combine sugar and cocoa in a saucepan. Whisk in milk; add butter. Bring to a boil over medium heat, stirring constantly. Remove from the heat; stir in vanilla. To serve, spoon about 2 tablespoons pie filling down the center of each crepe. Fold sides of crepe over filling; place in a greased 13-in. x 9-in. x 2-in. baking pan. Bake, uncovered, at 225° for 15 minutes. Transfer to serving plates; drizzle with warm chocolate sauce. **Yield:** 10 servings (20 crepes).

Editor's Note: Unfilled crepes may be covered and refrigerated for 2 to 3 days or frozen for 4 months.

1-1/2 teaspoons shortening, *divided*
   1/3 cup vanilla *or* **white chips**

In a heavy saucepan, heat caramels and water over low heat just until caramels are melted. Remove from the heat; cool slightly. Cut a thin slice from the bottom of each pear so it sits flat. Dip pears halfway in caramel; turn to coat and allow excess to drip off. Dip in nuts and place on a greased baking sheet; refrigerate for 30 minutes or until coating is firm.

In a heavy saucepan or microwave oven, melt chocolate chips with 1 teaspoon shortening; stir until smooth. In another saucepan, melt vanilla chips with remaining shortening; stir until smooth. Drizzle melted chips over pears and stems. Let stand until set. **Yield:** 6 servings.

*Editor's Note: This recipe was tested with Hershey caramels.

Chocolate Dessert Wraps

(Pictured above)

I came up with this chocolate and peanut butter treat when I needed a unique, fast dessert for a special dinner. The filled tortillas take just minutes on the grill and get a chewy consistency from marshmallows. — Laurie Gwaltney
Indianapolis, Indiana

1/2 cup creamy peanut butter*
   4 four tortillas (8 inches)
   1 cup miniature marshmallows
   1/2 cup miniature semisweet chocolate chips
Vanilla ice cream
Chocolate shavings, optional

Spread 2 tablespoons of peanut butter on each tortilla. Sprinkle 1/4 cup marshmallows and 2 tablespoons chocolate chips on half of each tortilla. Roll up, beginning with the topping side. Wrap each tortilla in heavy-duty foil; seal tightly.

Grill, covered, over low heat for 5-10 minutes or until heated through. Unwrap tortillas and place on dessert plates. Serve with ice cream. Garnish with chocolate shavings if desired. **Yield:** 4 servings.

*Editor's Note: Crunchy peanut butter is not recommended for this recipe.

Chocolate Dessert Waffles

(Pictured at right)

Warm from the iron, these fun-to-eat waffles can be dressed up in their "sundae" best. —Nanette Ehrsam
Wichita Falls, Texas

- 3/4 cup sugar
- 1/2 cup vegetable oil
- 2 eggs
- 1 teaspoon vanilla extract
- 1-1/4 cups all-purpose flour
- 6 tablespoons baking cocoa
- 1 teaspoon baking powder
- 1/2 teaspoon salt
- 1/2 teaspoon ground cinnamon
- Vanilla ice cream and caramel sauce, optional

In a bowl, combine sugar, oil, eggs and vanilla. Combine dry ingredients. Add to sugar mixture; mix well. Bake in a preheated waffle iron according to manufacturer's directions; remove carefully. Do not overbake. Serve warm with vanilla ice cream and caramel sauce if desired. **Yield:** 3-4 servings.

Chocolate and Fruit Trifle

(Pictured below)

This refreshing dessert layered with devil's food cake, a creamy pudding mixture, red berries and green kiwi is perfect for the holidays. I like making it in a clear glass trifle bowl to show off its festive colors. —Angie Dierikx
State Center, Iowa

- 1 package (18-1/4 ounces) devil's food cake mix
- 1 can (14 ounces) sweetened condensed milk
- 1 cup cold water
- 1 package (3.4 ounces) instant vanilla pudding mix
- 2 cups whipping cream, whipped

- 2 tablespoons orange juice
- 2 cups fresh strawberries, chopped
- 2 cups fresh raspberries
- 2 kiwifruit, peeled and chopped

Prepare cake batter according to package directions; pour into a greased 15-in. x 10-in. x 1-in. baking pan. Bake at 350° for 20 minutes or until a toothpick inserted near the center comes out clean. Cool completely on a wire rack. Crumble enough cake to measure 8 cups; set aside. (Save remaining cake for another use.)

In a mixing bowl, combine milk and water until smooth. Add pudding mix; beat on low for 2 minutes or until slightly thickened. Fold in whipped cream.

To assemble, spread 2-1/2 cups pudding mixture in a 4-qt. glass bowl. Top with half of the crumbled cake; sprinkle with 1 tablespoon orange juice. Arrange half of the berries and kiwi over cake. Repeat pudding and cake layers; sprinkle with remaining orange juice. Top with remaining pudding mixture. Spoon remaining fruit around edge of bowl. Cover and refrigerate until serving. **Yield:** 12-16 servings.

Chocolate Pudding Pizza

(Pictured on page 86)

My sister Brenda and I made up this recipe while talking on the phone. My family loved the classic pairing of chocolate and peanut butter presented in a whole new way.
—LaDonna Reed, Ponca City, Oklahoma

- 1 package (17-1/2 ounces) peanut butter cookie mix
- 1 carton (12 ounces) softened cream cheese
- 1-3/4 cups cold milk
- 1 package (3.9 ounces) instant chocolate pudding mix
- 1 carton (8 ounces) frozen whipped topping, thawed
- 1/4 cup miniature semisweet chocolate chips

Prepare cookie mix dough according to package directions. Press into a greased 12-in. pizza pan. Bake at 375° for 15 minutes or until set; cool. In a mixing bowl, beat cream cheese until smooth. Spread over crust. In another mixing bowl, beat milk and pudding mix on medium speed for 2 minutes. Spread over the cream cheese layer. Refrigerate for 20 minutes or until set. Spread with whipped topping. Sprinkle with chips. Chill for 1-2 hours. **Yield:** 12 servings.

Cream Puff Dessert

(Pictured below)

I recently took this rich dessert to a fellowship meeting at our church. Everyone loved it! In fact, so many people asked for the recipe that the church secretary printed it in our monthly newsletter.

—*Lisa Nash, Blaine, Minnesota*

> 1 cup water
> 1/2 cup butter (no substitutes)
> 1 cup all-purpose flour
> 4 eggs

FILLING:

> 1 package (8 ounces) cream cheese, softened
> 3-1/2 cups cold milk
> 2 packages (3.9 ounces *each*) instant chocolate pudding mix

TOPPING:

> 1 carton (8 ounces) frozen whipped topping, thawed
> 1/4 cup milk chocolate ice cream topping
> 1/4 cup caramel ice cream topping
> 1/3 cup chopped almonds

In a saucepan over medium heat, bring water and butter to a boil. Add flour all at once; stir until a smooth ball forms. Remove from heat; let stand for 5 minutes. Add eggs, one at a time, beating well after each addition. Beat until smooth. Spread into a greased 13-in. x 9-in. x 2-in. baking dish. Bake at 400° for 30-35 minutes or until puffed and golden brown. Cool completely on a wire rack.

Meanwhile, in a mixing bowl, beat cream cheese, milk and pudding mix until smooth. Spread over puff; refrigerate for 20 minutes. Spread with whipped topping; refrigerate until serving. Drizzle with chocolate and caramel toppings; sprinkle with almonds. Store leftovers in the refrigerator. **Yield:** 12 servings.

Chocolate Peanut Delight

(Pictured above)

Peanut lovers will appreciate this yummy dessert I dreamed up. A brownie-like crust is packed with nuts, topped with a fluffy peanut butter layer and covered with whipped topping and more nuts. It was so well received that I made it for a local restaurant where I used to work.

—*Karen Kutruff, New Berlin, Pennsylvania*

> 1 package (18-1/4 ounces) chocolate cake mix
> 1/2 cup butter *or* margarine, melted
> 1/4 cup milk
> 1 egg
> 1 cup chopped peanuts, *divided*
> 1 package (8 ounces) cream cheese, softened
> 1 cup peanut butter
> 1 cup confectioners' sugar
> 1 can (14 ounces) sweetened condensed milk
> 1-1/2 teaspoons vanilla extract
> 1 carton (16 ounces) frozen whipped topping, thawed, *divided*
> 1/2 cup semisweet chocolate chips
> 4-1/2 teaspoons butter *or* margarine
> 1/2 teaspoon vanilla extract

In a mixing bowl, combine dry cake mix, butter, milk and egg. Add 3/4 cup of peanuts. Spread into a greased 13-in. x 9-in. x 2-in. baking pan. Bake at 350° for 30 minutes or until a toothpick inserted near the center comes out clean. Cool on a wire rack.

In a mixing bowl, beat the cream cheese, peanut butter, sugar, condensed milk and vanilla until smooth. Fold in 3 cups whipped topping. Spread over the crust; top with the remaining whipped topping and peanuts.

In a microwave-safe bowl, heat chocolate chips and butter on high for 1 minute or until melted. Stir in vanilla until smooth; drizzle over cake. Refrigerate for 2-3 hours before cutting. **Yield:** 12-15 servings.

Rich Truffle Wedges

(Pictured above)

I've served this decadent dessert numerous times. It has a fudgy consistency and big chocolate taste. The tart raspberry sauce complements the flavor and looks lovely over each slice. —Patricia Vatta, Norwood, Ontario

    1/2 cup butter (no substitutes)
      6 squares (1 ounce *each*) semisweet chocolate, chopped
      3 eggs
    2/3 cup sugar
      1 teaspoon vanilla extract
    1/4 teaspoon salt
    2/3 cup all-purpose flour
GLAZE:
    1/4 cup butter
      2 squares (1 ounce *each*) semisweet chocolate
      2 squares (1 ounce *each*) unsweetened chocolate
      2 teaspoons honey
SAUCE:
      2 cups fresh *or* frozen unsweetened raspberries
      2 tablespoons sugar
Whipped cream, fresh raspberries and mint, optional

In a microwave oven or double boiler, melt butter and chocolate; stir until smooth. Cool for 10 minutes. In a mixing bowl, beat eggs, sugar, vanilla and salt until thick, about 4 minutes. Blend in chocolate mixture. Stir in flour; mix well. Pour into a greased and floured 9-in. springform pan. Bake at 350° for 25-30 minutes or until a toothpick inserted near the center comes out clean. Cool completely on a wire rack.

Combine glaze ingredients in a small saucepan; cook and stir over low heat until melted and smooth. Cool slightly. Run a knife around the edge of springform pan to loosen; remove cake to serving plate. Spread glaze over the top and sides; set aside.

For sauce, puree the raspberries in a blender or food processor. Press through a sieve if desired; discard seeds. Stir in sugar; chill until serving. Spoon sauce over individual servings. Garnish with whipped cream, raspberries and mint if desired. **Yield:** 12 servings.

Strawberry Chocolate Shortcake

(Pictured on page 86)

I like to make this luscious layered dessert for Valentine's Day. It's simple to prepare but so elegant and impressive. —Suzanne McKinley, Lyons, Georgia

3-1/2 cups biscuit/baking mix
    2/3 cup plus 2 teaspoons sugar, *divided*
    1/2 cup baking cocoa
      1 cup milk
    1/3 cup butter *or* margarine, melted
      1 egg white
2-1/2 pints fresh strawberries
      2 cups whipping cream
      3 tablespoons confectioners' sugar
      1 cup chocolate syrup

In a bowl, combine biscuit mix, 2/3 cup sugar and cocoa. Stir in milk and butter; mix well. Drop by 1/3 cupfuls at least 2 in. apart onto a greased baking sheet. Beat egg white until foamy; brush over shortcakes. Sprinkle with remaining sugar. Bake at 400° for 15-18 minutes. Cool on wire racks.

Set aside 10 whole strawberries; slice remaining strawberries. In a mixing bowl, beat cream and confectioners' sugar until soft peaks form. Just before serving, split shortcakes horizontally. Spoon half of the whipped cream and all of the sliced berries between cake layers. Spoon remaining whipped cream on top. Drizzle with chocolate syrup; top with a whole berry. **Yield:** 10 servings.

Mocha Fondue

(Pictured below)

People have such fun dipping pieces of cake and fruit into this glorious melted chocolate mixture. It's an exquisite treat to serve at wedding and baby showers or for another special gathering. I've found it to be a welcome part of any buffet. —Gloria Jarrett, Loveland, Ohio

3 cups milk chocolate chips
1/2 cup whipping cream
1 tablespoon instant coffee granules
2 tablespoons hot water
1 teaspoon vanilla extract
1/8 teaspoon ground cinnamon
1 pound cake (16 ounces), cut into 1-inch cubes
Strawberries, kiwi *or* other fresh fruit

In a heavy saucepan, melt chocolate with cream over low heat, stirring constantly. Dissolve coffee in water; add to chocolate mixture with vanilla and cinnamon. Mix well. Serve warm, using cake pieces and fruit for dipping. **Yield:** 2 cups.

White Chocolate Parfaits

(Pictured below)

This dressed-up dessert is great served on a warm summer night or at a dinner party. You can substitute other types of berries until you find your favorite combination.
—Jennifer Eilts, Central City, Nebraska

3/4 cup whipping cream
1/4 cup sugar
2 teaspoons cornstarch
2 egg yolks
4 squares (1 ounce *each*) white baking chocolate
1 teaspoon vanilla extract
3 cups whipped topping
1-1/2 cups fresh blueberries
1-1/2 cups fresh raspberries
Sliced strawberries and additional whipped topping, optional

In a saucepan, heat the cream just to a boil. In a bowl, combine sugar and cornstarch; stir in yolks until combined. Stir a small amount of hot cream into yolk mixture; return all to pan. Cook and stir for 2 minutes or until mixture reaches 160° and is thickened. Stir in chocolate until melted; add vanilla. Cool to room temperature,

about 15 minutes. Fold in whipped topping. Place 1/4 cup each in four parfait glasses. Combine blueberries and raspberries; place 1/4 cup in each glass. Repeat layers of chocolate mixture and berries twice. Cover and refrigerate for at least 1 hour. Garnish with strawberries and whipped topping if desired. **Yield:** 4 servings.

Chocolate-Filled Cream Puffs

(Pictured above)

This is a heavenly dessert for chocolate lovers. Each puff is stuffed with chocolate cream and drizzled with chocolate glaze. *—Kathy Kittell, Lenexa, Kansas*

1 cup water
6 tablespoons butter (no substitutes)
1 cup all-purpose flour
1/4 teaspoon salt
4 eggs
FILLING:
1 cup whipping cream
1/2 cup confectioners' sugar
2 tablespoons baking cocoa
GLAZE:
1 square (1 ounce) unsweetened chocolate
1 tablespoon butter
1/2 cup confectioners' sugar
2 tablespoons water

In a saucepan over medium heat, bring water and butter to a boil. Add flour and salt all at once; stir until a smooth ball forms. Remove from the heat; let stand 5 minutes. Add eggs, one at a time, beating well after each. Beat until smooth. Cover a baking sheet with foil; grease foil. Drop batter into six mounds onto foil. Bake at 400° for 15 minutes. Reduce heat to 350°; bake 30 minutes longer.

Remove puffs to a wire rack. Immediately cut a slit in each for steam to escape. In a mixing bowl, beat cream until soft peaks form. Gradually add sugar and cocoa, beating until almost stiff. Split puffs and remove soft dough. Add filling; replace tops. Melt chocolate and butter; stir in sugar and water. Drizzle over puffs. Chill. **Yield:** 6 servings.

Chocolate Cobbler

(Pictured at right)

It's impossible to resist the flavorful chocolate sauce that appears when this delightful cake bakes.
—Margaret McNeil, Memphis, Tennessee

    1 cup self-rising flour*
    1/2 cup sugar
    2 tablespoons plus 1/4 cup baking cocoa, *divided*
    1/2 cup milk
    3 tablespoons vegetable oil
    1 cup packed brown sugar
1-3/4 cups hot water
Vanilla ice cream, optional

In a bowl, combine the flour, sugar and 2 tablespoons cocoa. Stir in milk and oil until smooth. Pour into a greased 8-in. square baking pan. Combine the brown sugar and remaining cocoa; sprinkle over batter. Pour hot water over top (do not stir). Bake at 350° for 40-45 minutes or until top of cake springs back when lightly touched. Serve warm with ice cream if desired. **Yield:** 6-8 servings.

   *Editor's Note: As a substitute for self-rising flour, place 1-1/2 teaspoons baking powder and 1/2 teaspoon salt in a measuring cup. Add all-purpose flour to measure 1 cup.

Chocolate Cherry Torte

(Pictured below)

Mom has made this sweet treat for years. Since she knows how much my sister and I like it, she's still happy to serve this torte when we're home for a meal. The chocolate-covered graham cracker crust and fluffy filling are extra-special. —Sue Gronholz, Columbus, Wisconsin

    1 pound chocolate-covered graham cracker
        cookies (56 cookies), crushed
    1 cup butter *or* margarine, melted

    2 envelopes whipped topping mix
    1 cup cold milk
    1 teaspoon vanilla extract
    1 package (8 ounces) cream cheese, softened
    2 cans (21 ounces *each*) cherry pie filling

Set aside 1/4 cup crushed cookies for topping. Combine the remaining cookies with butter; spread into a 13-in. x 9-in. x 2-in. dish. Set aside. In a mixing bowl, combine whipped topping mixes, milk and vanilla; beat on low speed until blended. Beat on high for 4 minutes or until thickened and stiff peaks form. Add cream cheese; beat until smooth. Spread over crust; top with pie filling. Sprinkle with reserved cookies. Refrigerate for 12-24 hours before serving. **Yield:** 12-16 servings.

Valentine Berries and Cream

(Pictured on page 86)

Everyone was so impressed with this scrumptious filled chocolate heart served at a banquet held by our adult Sunday school class. I got the recipe, and now I enjoy rave reviews from family and friends when I serve it.
—Tamera O'Sullivan, Apple Valley, Minnesota

    8 squares (1 ounce *each*) semisweet chocolate
    1 tablespoon shortening
    2 packages (3 ounces *each*) cream cheese,
        softened
  1/4 cup butter *or* margarine, softened
1-1/2 cups confectioners' sugar
  1/3 cup baking cocoa
    2 tablespoons milk
    1 teaspoon vanilla extract
2-1/2 cups whipping cream, whipped, *divided*
1-1/2 cups fresh strawberries, halved

Line a 9-in. heart-shaped or square baking pan with foil; set aside. In a heavy saucepan over low heat, melt chocolate and shortening; stir until smooth. Pour into prepared pan, swirling to coat the bottom and 1-1/2 in. up the sides. Refrigerate for 1 minute, then swirl the chocolate to

reinforce sides of heart or box. Refrigerate for 30 minutes or until firm. Using foil, lift from pan; remove foil and place chocolate heart on a serving plate.

In a mixing bowl, beat the cream cheese and butter until smooth. Combine confectioners' sugar and cocoa; add to creamed mixture with milk and vanilla. Beat until smooth. Gently fold two-thirds of the whipped cream into cream cheese mixture. Spoon into heart. Insert star tip #32 into a pastry or plastic bag; fill with the remaining whipped cream. Pipe around the edge of heart. Garnish with strawberries. **Yield:** 8-10 servings.

Frozen Mocha Torte

(Pictured below)

For an easy, make-ahead dessert that's elegant and luscious, try this recipe that my mom has used for years. This torte has the perfect blend of mocha and chocolate in each cool refreshing slice. —Lisa Kivirist
Browntown, Wisconsin

1-1/4 cups chocolate wafer crumbs (about 24 wafers), divided
1/4 cup sugar
1/4 cup butter *or* margarine, melted
1 package (8 ounces) cream cheese, softened
1 can (14 ounces) sweetened condensed milk
2/3 cup chocolate syrup
2 tablespoons instant coffee granules
1 tablespoon hot water
1 cup whipping cream, whipped
Chocolate-covered coffee beans, optional

Combine 1 cup wafer crumbs, sugar and butter. Press onto the bottom and 1 in. up the sides of a greased 9-in. springform pan; set aside. In a mixing bowl, beat cream cheese, milk and chocolate syrup until smooth. Dissolve coffee granules in hot water; add to cream cheese mixture. Fold in whipped cream. Pour over the crust. Sprinkle with remaining crumbs. Cover and freeze for 8 hours or overnight. Uncover and remove from the freezer 10-15 minutes before serving. Garnish with coffee beans if desired. **Yield:** 10-12 servings.

Chocolate-Filled Meringue

(Pictured above)

This is my favorite dessert for the Christmas season. It has a nutty, chewy crust and dark chocolate filling that's not too sweet. I'm proud to serve it, and my guests love the rich taste. —Joan Totton, Stanfield, Oregon

3 egg whites
1/2 teaspoon vanilla extract
1/4 teaspoon cream of tartar
1/4 teaspoon salt
1/2 cup sugar
1/4 cup confectioners' sugar
3/4 cup finely chopped pecans
1 cup (6 ounces) semisweet chocolate chips, optional
FILLING:
2 milk chocolate candy bars (1.55 ounces *each*)
1 square (1 ounce) unsweetened chocolate
1/4 cup water
1 teaspoon vanilla extract
1 cup whipping cream, whipped
Additional whipped cream, optional

In a mixing bowl, beat egg whites, vanilla, cream of tartar and salt until soft peaks form. Gradually add sugars, beating until stiff peaks form. Fold in pecans. Grease the bottom and sides of a 9-in. pie plate, leaving top edge ungreased. Spread meringue onto the bottom and up the sides of prepared plate. Build up top edge. Bake at 350° for 20-30 minutes or until lightly browned. Cool on a wire rack.

If chocolate stars are desired, melt chocolate chips. Transfer chocolate to a small heavy-duty resealable plastic bag; cut a small hole in one corner of bag. On a waxed paper-lined baking sheet, pipe chocolate into star shapes. Refrigerate until firm, about 15 minutes. When ready to serve, carefully remove stars with a metal spatula.

For filling, in a heavy saucepan, combine candy bars, unsweetened chocolate and water. Cook and stir over low heat until melted. Pour into a large bowl; cool to room temperature. Stir in vanilla. Fold in whipped cream; pour into the crust. Top with additional whipped cream and chocolate stars if desired. **Yield:** 6-8 servings.

CANDY BAR CROISSANTS, PAGE 100

CHOCOLATE CHIP COFFEE RING, PAGE 98

TRIPLE-CHOCOLATE QUICK BREAD, PAGE 101

CHOCOLATE COOKIE MUFFINS, PAGE 102

Breads & Muffins

Cocoa Macaroon Muffins

(Pictured above)

This recipe is an old-time favorite that I've modified over the years depending on whether I served them for breakfast, a snack or as dessert. I love chocolate in any form, and these muffins pair it with coconut for a yummy result.
—Carol Wilson, Rio Rancho, New Mexico

    2 cups all-purpose flour
  1/2 cup sugar
    3 tablespoons baking cocoa
    3 teaspoons baking powder
    1 teaspoon salt
    1 cup milk
    1 egg
  1/3 cup vegetable oil
1-1/4 cups flaked coconut, *divided*
  1/4 cup sweetened condensed milk
  1/4 teaspoon almond extract

In a bowl, combine flour, sugar, cocoa, baking powder and salt. Combine milk, egg and oil; mix well. Stir into dry ingredients just until moistened. Spoon 2 tablespoonfuls into 12 greased or paper-lined muffin cups.

Combine 1 cup coconut, condensed milk and extract; place 2 teaspoonfuls in the center of each cup (do not spread). Top with remaining batter; sprinkle with remaining coconut. Bake at 400° for 20-22 minutes or until muffins test done. Cool for 5 minutes before removing from pan to a wire rack. **Yield:** 1 dozen.

Chocolate Zucchini Bread

You'd never guess zucchini is the "secret ingredient" in this easy-to-assemble bread—it has such big chocolate taste! I freeze extra zucchini from my garden in summer and make this bread to give as gifts all winter long.
—Charlotte McDaniel, Williamsville, Illinois

    3 cups all-purpose flour
    3 cups sugar
  1/2 cup baking cocoa

1-1/2 teaspoons baking powder
1-1/2 teaspoons baking soda
    1 teaspoon salt
  1/4 teaspoon ground cinnamon
    4 eggs
1-1/2 cups vegetable oil
    2 tablespoons butter *or* margarine, melted
1-1/2 teaspoons vanilla extract
1-1/2 teaspoons almond extract
    3 cups grated zucchini
    1 cup chopped pecans
  1/2 cup raisins

In a large bowl, combine the first seven ingredients. Combine the eggs, oil, butter and extracts; mix well. Stir into dry ingredients just until moistened. Fold in zucchini, pecans and raisins. Pour into three greased and floured 8-in. x 4-in. x 2-in. loaf pans. Bake at 350° for 55-60 minutes or until a toothpick inserted near the center comes out clean. Cool for 10 minutes; remove from the pans to wire racks. **Yield:** 3 loaves.

Chocolate Chip Coffee Ring

(Pictured below and on page 96)

When I was a girl, my mother served this only once a year—for Christmas-morning brunch. But it could easily be served as dessert besides or as a snack packed in a lunch. It travels very well. Sometimes when I bake this just for my husband and me, I'll prepare two bread pans' worth and freeze one.
—Laura Hertel
Columbia, Missouri

  1/2 cup butter *or* margarine, softened
    1 cup sugar
    2 eggs
    1 cup (8 ounces) sour cream
    1 teaspoon vanilla extract
    2 cups all-purpose flour
    1 teaspoon baking powder
    1 teaspoon baking soda
  1/2 teaspoon salt
  3/4 cup semisweet chocolate chips
TOPPING:
  1/2 cup all-purpose flour
  1/2 cup packed brown sugar

1-1/2 teaspoons baking cocoa
  1/4 cup cold butter *or* margarine
  1/2 cup chopped pecans
  1/4 cup semisweet chocolate chips

In a mixing bowl, cream butter and sugar until fluffy. Beat in eggs. Add sour cream and vanilla; mix just until combined. Set aside. Combine flour, baking powder, baking soda and salt; add to creamed mixture. Stir in the chocolate chips. Pour into a greased 8-cup fluted tube pan.

For topping, combine flour, sugar and cocoa; cut in butter until mixture resembles coarse crumbs. Stir in pecans and chocolate chips. Sprinkle over batter. Bake at 350° for 55-60 minutes or until a toothpick inserted near the center comes out clean. Cool in pan 20 minutes before removing to a wire rack to cool completely. **Yield:** 8-10 servings.

Editor's Note: A greased 9-in. square baking pan can be used instead of the 8-cup fluted tube pan; bake for 45-50 minutes.

S'more Jumbo Muffins

(Pictured above)

My daughter loves marshmallows, graham crackers and chocolate, so I came up with this muffin just for her. My whole family gobbles them up! Each bite reminds us of camping out. —Pam Ivbuls, Omaha, Nebraska

1-1/2 cups all-purpose flour
  1/2 cup graham cracker crumbs (about 8 squares)
  1/4 cup packed brown sugar
    1 teaspoon baking soda
  1/2 teaspoon salt
    1 egg
1-1/2 cups buttermilk
  1/4 cup vegetable oil
  3/4 cup semisweet chocolate chips
1-1/4 cups miniature marshmallows, *divided*

In a large bowl, combine all of the dry ingredients. Combine egg, buttermilk and oil; mix well. Stir into the dry ingredients just until moistened. Fold in the chocolate

chips and 1 cup marshmallows.

Fill greased jumbo muffin cups three-fourths full. Sprinkle with remaining marshmallows. Bake at 375° for 18-20 minutes or until a toothpick inserted near the center comes out clean. Cool for 5 minutes before removing from pan to a wire rack. Serve warm. **Yield:** 6 muffins.

Pumpkin Chocolate Loaf

(Pictured below)

These moist chocolate loaves, with a hint of pumpkin and spice, have been a favorite for years. They can be sliced to serve as snacks or dessert. —Kathy Gardner
Rockville, Maryland

3-1/2 cups sugar
1-1/4 cups vegetable oil
    3 eggs
    1 can (29 ounces) solid-pack pumpkin
    3 squares (1 ounce *each*) unsweetened chocolate, melted and cooled
1-1/2 teaspoons vanilla extract
3-3/4 cups all-purpose flour
1-1/2 teaspoons salt
1-1/2 teaspoons baking powder
1-1/4 teaspoons baking soda
1-1/4 teaspoons ground cinnamon
    1 to 1-1/4 teaspoons ground cloves
  1/2 teaspoon ground nutmeg
    2 cups (12 ounces) semisweet chocolate chips

In a large bowl, combine sugar and oil. Add eggs; mix well. Stir in the pumpkin, chocolate and vanilla; mix well. Combine the dry ingredients; stir into pumpkin mixture just until blended. Stir in chips.

Transfer to three greased 9-in. x 5-in. x 3-in. loaf pans. Bake at 350° for 55-65 minutes or until a toothpick inserted near the center comes out clean. Cool for 10 minutes before removing from pans to wire racks. **Yield:** 3 loaves.

Chocolate Chip Carrot Bread

(Pictured at right)

My family likes sweet breads, and this loaf incorporates many of their favorite ingredients. I'm a former newspaper food columnist, and coming up with flavorful recipes that are a little out-of-the-ordinary is a favorite pastime.
—Sharon Setzer, Philomath, Oregon

- 3 cups all-purpose flour
- 1 cup sugar
- 1 cup packed brown sugar
- 2 to 3 teaspoons ground cinnamon
- 2 teaspoons baking powder
- 1 teaspoon baking soda
- 1 teaspoon salt
- 1 teaspoon ground ginger
- 1/4 to 1/2 teaspoon ground cloves
- 3 eggs
- 3/4 cup orange juice
- 3/4 cup vegetable oil
- 1 teaspoon vanilla extract
- 2 cups grated carrots
- 1 cup (6 ounces) semisweet chocolate chips

In a large bowl, combine the first nine ingredients. In a small bowl, beat the eggs, orange juice, oil and vanilla. Stir into the dry ingredients just until moistened. Fold in the carrots and chocolate chips.

Transfer to two greased 8-in. x 4-in. x 2-in. loaf pans. Bake at 350° for 55-60 minutes or until a toothpick inserted near the center comes out clean. Cool for 10 minutes before removing from pans to wire racks. **Yield:** 2 loaves.

Chocolate Chip Mini-Muffins

(Pictured below)

I bake a lot of different muffins, but I use this recipe the most. These little bitefuls are packed with lots of wonderful flavor. —Joanne Shew Chuk, St. Benedict, Saskatchewan

- 1/2 cup sugar
- 1/4 cup shortening
- 1 egg
- 1/2 cup milk
- 1/2 teaspoon vanilla extract
- 1 cup all-purpose flour
- 1/2 teaspoon baking soda
- 1/2 teaspoon baking powder
- 1/4 teaspoon salt
- 2/3 cup miniature semisweet chocolate chips

In a large mixing bowl, cream sugar and shortening until fluffy. Add egg, milk and vanilla; mix well. Combine dry ingredients. Gradually add to creamed mixture; mix well. Fold in chocolate chips.

Spoon about 1 tablespoon of batter into each greased or paper-lined mini-muffin cup. Bake at 375° for 10-13 minutes or until a toothpick inserted near the center comes out clean. Cool in pan 10 minutes before removing to a wire rack. **Yield:** about 3 dozen.

Candy Bar Croissants

(Pictured on page 96)

These croissants are a rich, buttery treat that combines convenient refrigerated crescent rolls and milk chocolate candy bars.
—Beverly Sterling, Gasport, New York

- 1 tube (8 ounces) refrigerated crescent rolls
- 1 tablespoon butter *or* margarine, softened
- 2 plain milk chocolate candy bars (1.55 ounces *each*), broken into small pieces
- 1 egg, beaten
- 2 tablespoons sliced almonds

Unroll crescent roll dough; separate into triangles. Brush with butter. Arrange candy bar pieces evenly over triangles; roll up from the wide end. Place point side down on a greased baking sheet; curve ends slightly. Brush with egg and sprinkle with almonds. Bake at 375° for 11-13 minutes or until golden brown. Cool on a wire rack. **Yield:** 8 servings.

Triple-Chocolate Quick Bread

(Pictured below and on page 96)

Every year around Christmas, I'll make this bread for my family. I've given it also as a homemade gift. It's pretty wrapped in colored foil or put in a tin.
—Karen Grimes, Stephens City, Virginia

1/2 cup butter *or* margarine, softened
2/3 cup packed brown sugar
2 eggs
1 cup (6 ounces) miniature semisweet
   chocolate chips, melted
1-1/2 cups applesauce
2 teaspoons vanilla extract
2-1/2 cups all-purpose flour
1 teaspoon baking powder
1 teaspoon baking soda
1 teaspoon salt
1/2 cup miniature semisweet chocolate chips
GLAZE:
1/2 cup miniature semisweet chocolate chips
1 tablespoon butter *or* margarine
2 to 3 tablespoons half-and-half cream
1/2 cup confectioners' sugar
1/4 teaspoon vanilla extract
Pinch salt

In a mixing bowl, cream butter and sugar. Add eggs and melted chocolate; mix well. Add applesauce and vanilla. Set aside. Combine flour, baking powder, baking soda and salt; add to creamed mixture and mix well. Stir in chocolate chips. Spoon the batter into four greased 5-1/2-in. x 3-in. x 2-in. loaf pans. Bake at 350° for 35-40 minutes or until a toothpick inserted near the center comes out clean. Cool in pans 10 minutes before removing to wire racks to cool completely.

For glaze, melt chocolate chips and butter in a saucepan; stir in cream. Remove from the heat; stir in sugar, vanilla and salt. Drizzle over warm bread. **Yield:** 4 mini loaves.

Buttermilk Chocolate Bread

(Pictured above)

I serve this rich cake-like bread and its creamy chocolate honey butter often at Christmastime. It makes a great brunch item, but it also goes well on a dinner buffet. This recipe won me a "Best in Category" award in a local cooking contest.
—Patrice Bruwer
Grand Rapids, Michigan

1/2 cup butter *or* margarine, softened
1 cup sugar
2 eggs
1-1/2 cups all-purpose flour
1/2 cup baking cocoa
1/2 teaspoon salt
1/2 teaspoon baking powder
1/2 teaspoon baking soda
1 cup buttermilk
1/3 cup chopped pecans
CHOCOLATE HONEY BUTTER:
1/2 cup butter (no substitutes), softened
2 tablespoons honey
2 tablespoons chocolate syrup

In a mixing bowl, cream butter and sugar. Add eggs, one at a time, beating well after each addition. Combine the flour, cocoa, salt, baking powder and baking soda; add to creamed mixture alternately with buttermilk. Fold in pecans.

Pour into a greased 9-in. x 5-in. x 3-in. loaf pan. Bake at 350° for 55-60 minutes or until a toothpick inserted near the center comes out clean. Cool for 10 minutes before removing from pan to a wire rack.

In a small mixing bowl, beat butter until fluffy. Add honey and chocolate syrup; mix well. Serve with the bread. **Yield:** 1 loaf (1/2 cup butter).

Chocolate Tea Bread

(Pictured above)

Applesauce is the secret ingredient that makes this cake-like loaf so moist. It's a success whenever I serve it.
—Dorothy Bateman, Carver, Massachusetts

  1/2 cup applesauce
  1/3 cup shortening
    2 eggs
  1/3 cup water
1-1/4 cups sugar
1-1/2 cups all-purpose flour
  1/3 cup baking cocoa
    1 teaspoon baking soda
  3/4 teaspoon salt
  1/4 teaspoon baking powder
    1 cup (6 ounces) semisweet chocolate chips
  1/3 cup chopped walnuts
GLAZE:
  1/2 cup confectioners' sugar
    1 to 2 tablespoons milk
  1/4 teaspoon vanilla extract
Pinch salt

In a mixing bowl, combine applesauce, shortening, eggs, water and sugar; beat on low for 30 seconds. Combine dry ingredients; add to applesauce mixture. Beat on low for 30 seconds. Beat on high for 2-1/2 minutes, scraping bowl occasionally. Fold in chocolate chips and nuts.

Pour into a greased and floured 9-in. x 5-in. x 3-in. loaf pan. Bake at 350° for 60-70 minutes or until a toothpick inserted in the center comes out clean. Cool in pan 10 minutes before removing to a wire rack to cool completely. Combine glaze ingredients; drizzle over bread. **Yield:** 1 loaf.

Double Chocolate Banana Muffins

Combining two great flavors makes these moist muffins doubly good. —Donna Brockett, Kingfisher, Oklahoma

1-1/2 cups all-purpose flour
    1 cup sugar
  1/4 cup baking cocoa

    1 teaspoon baking soda
  1/2 teaspoon salt
  1/4 teaspoon baking powder
1-1/3 cups mashed ripe bananas
  1/3 cup vegetable oil
    1 egg
    1 cup (6 ounces) miniature semisweet chocolate chips

In a large bowl, combine the first six ingredients. In a small bowl, combine bananas, oil and egg; stir into dry ingredients just until moistened. Fold in chocolate chips. Fill greased or paper-lined muffin cups three-fourths full. Bake at 350° for 20-25 minutes or until a toothpick inserted near the center comes out clean. **Yield:** about 1 dozen.

Chocolate Cookie Muffins

(Pictured below and on page 96)

I'm always on the lookout for new ways to make muffins. This fun version includes crushed cream-filled chocolate cookies in the batter. They're a double treat—like eating muffins and cookies at the same time. —Jan Blue
Cuyahoga Falls, Ohio

1-3/4 cups all-purpose flour
  1/4 cup sugar
    3 teaspoons baking powder
  1/3 cup cold butter *or* margarine
    1 egg
    1 cup milk
  16 cream-filled chocolate sandwich cookies, coarsely chopped
TOPPING:
    3 tablespoons all-purpose flour
    3 tablespoons sugar
    5 cream-filled chocolate sandwich cookies, finely crushed
    2 tablespoons cold butter *or* margarine
    1 cup vanilla chips
    1 tablespoon shortening

In a large bowl, combine flour, sugar and baking powder. Cut in butter until mixture resembles coarse crumbs. Beat egg and milk; stir into dry ingredients just until moistened. Fold in chopped cookies. Fill greased muffin cups two-thirds full.

For topping, combine the flour, sugar and crushed cookies. Cut in the butter until crumbly; sprinkle about 1 tablespoon over each muffin. Bake at 400° for 16-18 minutes or until muffins test done. Cool for 5 minutes before removing from pan to a wire rack. In a heavy saucepan over low heat, melt vanilla chips and shortening until smooth. Drizzle over cooled muffins. **Yield:** 1 dozen.

Cocoa Ripple Squares

(Pictured below)

When my four children were growing up, this was a frequent birthday treat. Now my grandchildren request it. It also could be served at a tea or at a card party.
—*Phyllis Rank, Wapato, Washington*

      1/2 cup shortening
        1 cup sugar, *divided*
        2 eggs
1-1/2 cups all-purpose flour
        2 teaspoons baking powder
      3/4 teaspoon salt
      2/3 cup milk
        2 tablespoons baking cocoa
      2/3 cup chopped walnuts, *divided*
        3 tablespoons butter *or* margarine

In a mixing bowl, cream shortening and 3/4 cup sugar. Add eggs; beat until light and fluffy. Combine the flour, baking powder and salt; add to creamed mixture alternately with milk, beating well after each addition. Set aside.

Combine cocoa, 1/3 cup walnuts and remaining sugar. Spoon a third of the batter into a greased 9-in. square baking pan. Sprinkle with half of the cocoa mixture. Dot with half of the butter. Repeat layers; top with remaining batter. Sprinkle with remaining walnuts. Bake at 350° for 35-40 minutes or until a toothpick inserted near the center comes out clean. Serve warm. **Yield:** 9 servings.

Cappuccino Muffins

(Pictured above)

These are my favorite muffins to serve with a cup of coffee or a tall glass of cold milk. Not only are they great for breakfast, they make a tasty dessert or midnight snack. I get lots of recipe requests whenever I serve them. The espresso spread is also super on a bagel. —*Janice Bassing Racine, Wisconsin*

ESPRESSO SPREAD:
        4 ounces cream cheese, cubed
        1 tablespoon sugar
      1/2 teaspoon instant coffee granules
      1/2 teaspoon vanilla extract
      1/4 cup miniature semisweet chocolate chips
MUFFINS:
        2 cups all-purpose flour
      3/4 cup sugar
2-1/2 teaspoons baking powder
        1 teaspoon ground cinnamon
      1/2 teaspoon salt
        1 cup milk
        2 tablespoons instant coffee granules
      1/2 cup butter *or* margarine, melted
        1 egg, beaten
        1 teaspoon vanilla extract
      3/4 cup miniature semisweet chocolate chips

In a food processor or blender, combine the spread ingredients; cover and process until well blended. Cover and refrigerate until serving.

In a bowl, combine flour, sugar, baking powder, cinnamon and salt. In another bowl, stir milk and coffee granules until coffee is dissolved. Add butter, egg and vanilla; mix well. Stir into dry ingredients just until moistened. Fold in chocolate chips. Fill greased or paper-lined muffin cups two-thirds full. Bake at 375° for 17-20 minutes or until muffins test done. Cool for 5 minutes before removing from pans to wire racks. Serve with espresso spread. **Yield:** about 14 muffins (1 cup spread).

MOCHA PUNCH, PAGE 109

PUDDINGWICHES, PAGE 106

CHOCOLATE CHIP CHEESE BALL,
PAGE 107

CHERRY S'MORES, PAGE 108

Snacks & Beverages

Cocoa Munch Mix

(Pictured above)

This sweet snack is a nice change of pace from the typical cookies and brownies found at bake sales. Packed in resealable bags, it always goes fast. It's great for camping trips, too. —Amanda Denton, Barre, Vermont

    4 cups Cheerios
    4 cups Chex
    1 cup slivered almonds
    2 tablespoons baking cocoa
    2 tablespoons sugar
  1/2 cup butter *or* margarine, melted
    1 cup raisins
    1 package (12 ounces) vanilla *or* white chips

In a large bowl, combine the cereals and almonds. In a small bowl, combine cocoa, sugar and butter. Pour over cereal mixture and toss to coat. Pour into a greased 13-in. x 9-in. x 2-in. baking pan. Bake at 250° for 1 hour, stirring every 15 minutes. Cool completely. Stir in raisins and chips. **Yield:** 10 servings.

Puddingwiches

(Pictured on page 104)

Our daughter loves these fun chocolate and peanut butter snacks. I often defrost them in the microwave so they're a bit softer. —Joanne Zimmerman, Ephrata, Pennsylvania

1-1/2 cups cold milk
    1 package (3.9 ounces) instant chocolate
      pudding mix
  1/4 to 1/2 cup peanut butter
    15 whole graham crackers

In a mixing bowl, combine the milk, pudding mix and peanut butter. Beat on low speed for 2 minutes. Let stand for 5 minutes. Break or cut graham crackers in half. Spread pudding mixture over half of the crackers; top with the remaining crackers. Wrap and freeze until firm. May be frozen for up to 1 month. **Yield:** 15 servings.

White Hot Chocolate

This creamy hot drink is smooth and soothing with a hint of spice. —Debbi Smith, Crossett, Arkansas

    3 cups half-and-half cream, *divided*
  2/3 cup vanilla *or* white chips
    1 cinnamon stick (3 inches)
  1/8 teaspoon ground nutmeg
    1 teaspoon vanilla extract
  1/4 teaspoon almond extract
Ground cinnamon, optional

In a saucepan, combine 1/4 cup cream, vanilla chips, cinnamon stick and nutmeg. Stir over low heat until chips are melted; discard cinnamon. Add remaining cream; stir until heated through. Remove from the heat; add extracts. Sprinkle each serving with ground cinnamon if desired. **Yield:** 4 servings.

Rocky Road Fudge Pops

(Pictured below)

These sweet frozen treats are simple to prepare and guaranteed to bring out the kid in anyone. The creamy pops feature a special chocolate and peanut topping. —Karen Grant, Tulare, California

    1 package (3.4 ounces) cook-and-serve chocolate
      pudding mix
2-1/2 cups milk
  1/2 cup chopped peanuts
  1/2 cup miniature semisweet chocolate chips
    12 plastic cups (3 ounces *each*)
  1/2 cup marshmallow creme
    12 Popsicle sticks

In a large microwave-safe bowl, combine pudding mix and milk. Microwave, uncovered, on high for 6 to 7-1/2 minutes or until bubbly and slightly thickened, stirring every 2 minutes. Cool for 20 minutes, stirring several times. Meanwhile, combine peanuts and chocolate chips; place about 2 tablespoons in each plastic cup. Stir marshmallow creme into pudding; spoon into cups. Insert Popsicle sticks; freeze. **Yield:** 12 servings.

Editor's Note: This recipe was tested in an 850-watt microwave.

Chocolate Cream Fruit Dip

(Pictured above)

My sweet mixture has a mild chocolate flavor that's especially good on strawberries. This recipe is truly an accident. While hosting a party, I realized I'd forgotten the fruit dip. So I raided my cabinets and put this combination together. It was a surprising success and has since become one of our family's favorites. —Debbie Bond, Richwood, West Virginia

  1 package (8 ounces) cream cheese,
    softened
1/4 cup chocolate syrup
  1 jar (7 ounces) marshmallow creme
Apple wedges, fresh strawberries and banana chunks

In a small mixing bowl, beat cream cheese and chocolate syrup. Fold in marshmallow creme. Cover and refrigerate until serving. Serve with fruit. **Yield:** about 2 cups.

Chocolate Chip Cheese Ball

(Pictured on page 104)

Your guests are in for a sweet surprise when they try this unusual cheese ball...it tastes just like cookie dough! Rolled in chopped pecans, the chip-studded spread is wonderful on regular or chocolate graham crackers. I especially like it because it can be assembled in a wink.
               —Kelly Glascock, Syracuse, Missouri

  1 package (8 ounces) cream cheese, softened
1/2 cup butter (no substitutes), softened
1/4 teaspoon vanilla extract
3/4 cup confectioners' sugar
  2 tablespoons brown sugar
3/4 cup miniature semisweet chocolate chips
3/4 cup finely chopped pecans
Graham crackers

In a mixing bowl, beat the cream cheese, butter and vanilla until fluffy. Gradually add sugars; beat just until combined. Stir in chocolate chips. Cover and refrigerate for 2 hours.

    Place cream cheese mixture on a large piece of plastic wrap; shape into a ball. Refrigerate for at least 1 hour. Just before serving, roll cheese ball in pecans. Serve with graham crackers. **Yield:** 1 cheese ball (about 2 cups).

Chocolate Malts

(Pictured below)

I can whip up this decadent ice cream drink in just minutes. It's a favorite with kids after a day in the pool or for dessert after a barbecue.   *—Marion Lowery*
                             Medford, Oregon

3/4 cup milk
1/2 cup caramel ice cream topping
  2 cups chocolate ice cream, softened
  3 tablespoons malted milk powder
  2 tablespoons chopped pecans, optional
Grated chocolate, optional

In a blender, combine the first five ingredients; cover and process until blended. Pour into chilled glasses. Sprinkle with grated chocolate if desired. **Yield:** 2-1/2 cups.

Cherry Chip Shakes

If you like the flavor of chocolate-covered cherries, you'll love this tempting shake. It's sweet and satisfying.
—*Mary Green, Circle Pines, Minnesota*

    3 cups vanilla ice cream *or* frozen vanilla yogurt
    3 tablespoons hot fudge ice cream topping
    1/4 cup miniature chocolate chips
    4 maraschino cherries
Whipped topping and additional cherries

In a blender, combine ice cream, fudge topping, chocolate chips and cherries; cover and process until blended. Pour into tall glasses; top with a dollop of whipped topping and a cherry. **Yield:** 2 servings.

Old-Fashioned Chocolate Soda

(Pictured below)

We enjoy making this old-fashioned soda fountain specialty at home. Besides being a favorite treat for my grandchildren, it's entertainment. They love to watch the magic of the soda foaming up as they urge me to add more whipped topping.—*Dawn Sams, Grayslake, Illinois*

    6 tablespoons chocolate syrup
    2 tablespoons whipped cream in a can
2-1/2 cups cold carbonated water
    4 scoops ice cream of your choice
Additional whipped cream, optional

For each serving, place 3 tablespoons chocolate syrup in a 16-oz. glass. Stir in 1 tablespoon of whipped cream and 1-1/4 cups water until foamy. Add two scoops of ice cream. Top with additional whipped cream if desired. **Yield:** 2 servings.

Microwaving Chocolate

MELTING chocolate in a microwave oven is easy and convenient. Simply place the unwrapped chocolate squares or chips in a microwave-safe bowl.

For 1-ounce squares of unsweetened or semi-sweet chocolate, microwave on high for 1 minute. If unmelted chocolate remains when stirred, microwave an additional 30 seconds.

For a 10- to 12-ounce package of regular or miniature chocolate chips, microwave for 1-1/2 minutes on high, then an additional 15 seconds if unmelted chocolate remains.

Cherry S'mores

(Pictured on page 104)

If you like s'mores, you'll enjoy this dressed-up variation. Each open-face treat gets a boost of sweetness from cherry pie filling. —*Margery Bryan, Royal City, Washington*

    1 plain milk chocolate candy bar (7 ounces)
    8 graham cracker squares
    8 large marshmallows
    1 cup cherry pie filling

Divide chocolate into eight pieces; place a piece on each graham cracker. Top with a marshmallow. Place two crackers at a time on a microwave-safe plate. Microwave on high for 15-35 seconds or until chocolate is melted and marshmallow is puffed. Top each with 1 tablespoon pie filling. **Yield:** 8 servings.

    Editor's Note: This recipe was tested in an 850-watt microwave.

Sweet Snack Mix

Tempt your troops with a twist on caramel corn. When I set out this nutty snack, the bowl empties fast.
—*Dee Georgiou, Omaha, Nebraska*

    14 cups popped popcorn
    3 cups crisp rice cereal
    2 cups salted peanuts
    1 pound white candy coating
    3 tablespoons creamy peanut butter

In a large bowl, combine popcorn, cereal and peanuts. In the top of a double boiler over simmering water, melt candy coating and peanut butter, stirring occasionally. Pour over popcorn mixture; stir to coat. Spread evenly on waxed paper. Allow to set for at least 2 hours. Store in an airtight container. **Yield:** 5-6 quarts.

Chocolate Pizza

(Pictured at right)

People who love chocolate will enjoy this delightfully sweet confection. —Janet Smith
Sunnyvale, California

3 cups vanilla *or* white chips, *divided*
2 cups (12 ounces) semisweet chocolate chips
2 cups miniature marshmallows
1 cup Rice Krispies
1 cup chopped walnuts
1/2 cup halved maraschino cherries, patted dry
1/4 cup flaked coconut
1 teaspoon vegetable oil

In a microwave-safe bowl, combine 2-1/2 cups vanilla chips and the chocolate chips. Microwave on high for 2 minutes; stir. Microwave for 1-2 minutes; stir until smooth. Immediately add marshmallows, cereal and walnuts; mix well.

Spread evenly on a 13-in. pizza pan that has been coated with nonstick cooking spray. Arrange cherries on top; sprinkle with coconut. Microwave the remaining vanilla chips on high for 1 minute. Add oil and stir until smooth. Drizzle over pizza. Chill until firm. Serve at room temperature. **Yield:** 16-20 servings.

Editor's Note: This recipe was tested in a 700-watt microwave.

Chocolate Caramel Apples

(Pictured below)

Caramel apples get dressed up for Halloween with chocolate, nuts and toffee bits. Cut into wedges, these scrumptious apples are easy to share. —Linda Smith
Frederick, Maryland

1 package (14 ounces) caramels
2 tablespoons water
4 wooden sticks

4 large tart apples
2 cups chopped pecans *or* peanuts
1 cup (6 ounces) semisweet chocolate chips
1 teaspoon shortening
1 cup English toffee bits *or* almond brickle chips

In a microwave-safe bowl, combine the caramels and water. Microwave, uncovered, on high for 1 minute; stir. Microwave 30-45 seconds longer or until the caramels are melted. Insert wooden sticks into apples; dip apples into the caramel mixture, turning to coat. Coat with nuts; set on waxed paper to cool.

Melt chocolate chips and shortening; drizzle over apples. Sprinkle with toffee bits. Set on waxed paper to cool. Cut into wedges to serve. **Yield:** 8 servings.

Editor's Note: This recipe was tested with Hershey caramels in an 850-watt microwave.

Mocha Punch

(Pictured on page 104)

I first tried this smooth, creamy punch at a friend's Christmas open house. It was so special and distinctive, I didn't leave until I had the recipe. —Yvonne Hatfield
Norman, Oklahoma

1-1/2 quarts water
1/2 cup instant chocolate drink mix
1/2 cup sugar
1/4 cup instant coffee granules
1/2 gallon vanilla ice cream
1/2 gallon chocolate ice cream
1 cup whipping cream, whipped
Chocolate curls, optional

In a large saucepan, bring water to a boil. Remove from the heat. Add drink mix, sugar and coffee; stir until dissolved. Cover and refrigerate for 4 hours or overnight.

About 30 minutes before serving, pour into a punch bowl. Add vanilla and chocolate ice cream by scoopfuls; stir until partially melted. Garnish with dollops of whipped cream and chocolate curls if desired. **Yield:** 20-25 servings (about 5 quarts).

Index